Citizenship and Language Learning:
international perspectives

Citizenship and Language Learning: international perspectives

Audrey Osler and Hugh Starkey

BRITISH COUNCIL *tb*

Trentham Books

Stoke on Trent, UK and Sterling, USA

in partnership with the British Council

Trentham Books Limited
Westview House   22883 Quicksilver Drive
734 London Road   Sterling
Oakhill   VA 20166-2012
Stoke on Trent   USA
Staffordshire
England ST4 5NP

First published 2005

British Library Cataloguing-in-Publication Data
A catalogue record for this book is available from the British Library

ISBN-13: 978-1-85856-334-3
ISBN-10: 1-85856-334-8

Cover photographs by Audrey Osler

Designed and typeset by Trentham Print Design Ltd, Chester and printed in
Great Britain by Bemrose Shafron (Printers) Ltd, Chester

Contents

Foreword

I am delighted to have this opportunity to introduce *Citizenship and Language Learning,* which addresses the growing importance of relating the teaching of English to the practical application of human rights and citizenship. This volume is the result of a British Council seminar on language and citizenship, which, in turn, has drawn on the strength of our work in English and Governance.

The British Council has worked to promote and improve the teaching of English since it was founded in 1934. Indeed, it was one of the principle objectives outlined in our Royal Charter of 1940. Initially, the language was seen as an asset in itself and also as a vehicle to carry the best of the values of the United Kingdom as expressed through our great literature. English lecturers would teach the present perfect tense and lecture on Hamlet in quick succession and with equal aplomb. Over the last few years, though, our work in English has become more closely linked to our work in other areas, especially our Governance programme. This has been a natural and very welcome development. After all, language is used for communication. And in today's schools and colleges, where there is an emphasis on interaction and exchange, the school language classroom provides a non-threatening context in which to discuss topics of concern to children and adolescents.

Through some of our projects in East and Central Europe and around the world, we have specifically encouraged the implementation of English Language curricula which include human rights and citizenship education topics. Students are doubly motivated by the benefit of approaching issues that are part of their lives and of crucial importance for humankind, and of improving their English language skills. What is more, the methodology that we use in teaching and training people to teach English of itself encourages dialogue, openness and respect. Teacher training, textbook and curricular reform have also been accompanied by initiatives to develop the use of drama in and outside the classroom, student project work and creative writing. Such initiatives involve not only the use of language *per se* but also the development of team-work, leadership, negotiating and presentation skills necessary, for example, to stage a school play in a local theatre. These are useful skills for responsible citizenship.

It seems quite natural, therefore, that one of our country teams took the next logical step in deciding to work with teachers to write a textbook on human rights. Published in Romania in 2003 and featured at the seminar and in this volume (chapter nine), *Rights Indeed* enables teachers to use the classroom to explore ethical issues behind everyday behaviour on the one hand and to make the 'big' concerns of today's world accessible to school students on the other.

Through our work with Ministries of Education and with teachers and trainers, the British Council has encouraged teachers to think of teaching as an enabling process, to view their students as complete human beings whom they can develop as part of the process of helping them learn the language. Dialogue, interaction, understanding, and the ability to adopt complex ap-proaches to difficult issues go hand in hand with reading, listening, writing and speaking. At the same time, the teachers themselves develop their own skills as team members and leaders; their sense of professional pride grows and they realise that they are themselves important parts of society. They have a sense of being members of a national, regional and global network. Essentially, they have moved from being passive recipients of the instructions of those above them in the social hierarchy to being active citizens with in-fluence on the future of their societies.

Citizenship is not, of course, assumed or enacted by an individual in isola-tion. It is all to do with how we relate to other individuals, to groups within our society and to other societies. And the British Council has been instru-mental in bringing people together from many groups within a region and even from far away regions. With the support of the Hornby Educational Trust, we have done this through regional training schools in many parts of the world. Some of these schools, for instance in Sri Lanka, Uzbekistan, Kazakhstan and Hungary, have chosen to focus specifically on intercultural dialogue, multiculturalism and different aspects of citizenship. Even where schools have dealt with other topics, they have acted as fora within which teachers from a variety of countries have learned to listen to one another with respect, despite any political differences that might divide them. The schools have highlighted the value of individual cultures, teaching pride in one's identity, while encouraging dialogue with other cultures and interaction with them. English is used as a *lingua franca* that allows barriers to be crossed and for speakers to realise their place in the wider regional and global community.

Another significant example of our work over the last few years has been the Peacekeeping English Project, in which we have worked with Ministries of Defence and of Internal Affairs. This project has not only been concerned with language improvement. It has contributed to national and international stability and security by increasing the capability of national forces to communicate and co-operate with each other, whilst facilitating the processes of re-structuring, demilitarisation and democratisation.

The British Council Seminars *Language Teaching and Citizenship Education* event brought together several strands of activity: the English Language Teaching Contacts Scheme, the Hornby Educational Trust programme, Peacekeeping English and projects in Romania, Pakistan, Sri Lanka and elsewhere. This event and this book, which marks an important stage in the dissemination of the ideas generated there, have shown how language teaching contributes to different understandings of citizenship and human rights at local, national and global levels.

I would particularly like to thank Audrey Osler and Hugh Starkey, formerly of the University of Leicester's Centre for Citizenship Studies in Education, who co-directed the seminar and have edited this book, and my colleagues Chris Palmer, Jeremy Jacobson and their teams for their work on this project.

David Green
Director
The British Council

Acknowledgements

We would like to thank a number of people who have supported us in the preparation of this book.

Chris Palmer and colleagues at the British Council in the UK for planning the seminar *Language Teaching and Citizenship Education in International Contexts* and supporting this publication.

Lena Milosevic and Ernesto Cussianovich at the British Council in Buenos Aires for hosting Audrey in Argentina and providing insights into the Multilingual Primary Schools project and education for children's rights.

Colleagues at the Centre for Citizenship Studies in Education at the University of Leicester. Barbara Hall for helping us to prepare for the British Council seminar and for liaising with participants and contributors.

Colleagues at the Centre for Citizenship and Human Rights Education at the University of Leeds. Especially Julie Hastings for assisting in the preparation of the type-script.

Gillian Klein of Trentham Books for her support and patience as we worked to realise this project.

Audrey Osler and Hugh Starkey

Acronyms and abbreviations

AILA	International Association of Applied Linguistics
AIMAV	International Association for the Development of Cross-Cultural Communication
BBC	British Broadcasting Corporation
BC	British Council
CE	Citizenship Education
CRC	UN Convention on the Rights of the Child 1989
DfEE	Department for Education and Employment
DfES	Department for Education and Skills
EAP	English for Academic Purposes
EDC	Education for Democratic Citizenship
ECHR	European Convention for the Protection of Human Rights and Fundamental Freedoms
EFL	English as a Foreign Language
ELT	English Language Teaching
ENIS	European Network of Innovative Schools
ESL	English as a Second Language
ESP	English for Specific Purposes
ESR	Educators for Social Responsibility
EST	English for Science and Technology
EU	European Union
FIPLA	World Federation of Modern Language Associations
FL	Foreign Language
GCBA	Government of the City of Buenos Aires
GCSE	General Certificate of Secondary Education
HRE	Human Rights Education
ICCPR	International Covenant on Civil and Political Rights

ICESCR International Covenant on Economic Social and Cultural Rights

ICT   Information and Communications Technology

IEARN   International Education and Resource Network

IFFTU   International Federation of Free Teacher Unions

JALT   Japan Association of Language Teaching

L2   Second Language

LIOJ   Language Institute of Japan

LSP   Languages for Specific Purposes

NGO   Non-Governmental Organisation

QCA   Qualifications and Curriculum Authority

REACP   Reading English Across the Curriculum Programme

SL   Second Language

TESOL   Teaching English to Speakers of Other Languages

UDHR   Universal Declaration of Human Rights 1948

UN   United Nations

UNA   United Nations Association

UNDP   United Nations Development Programme

UNESCO United Nations Educational Scientific and Cultural Organisation

UNICEF United Nations Children's Fund

WCOTP   World Confederation of Organisations of the Teaching Profession

Preface

Audrey Osler and Hugh Starkey

Throughout the world there is a growing interest among language teachers in how they might support their students in developing the skills to become effective citizens. At the same time there is, internationally, increased discussion and debate about citizenship and identity and about the ways we might educate citizens in multicultural contexts and in the context of an increasingly interdependent, yet unequal, world.

In 2003, the British Council hosted a seminar entitled *Language Teaching and Citizenship Education in International Contexts* which was attended by teachers, lecturers, researchers and administrators from some twenty countries in Africa, Asia, Europe, the Middle East and Latin America. Many more participants from across the world participated in the seminar by joining a concurrent online discussion group. *Citizenship and Language Learning: international perspectives* builds on the experiences of those who took part in the seminar, drawing on the presenters' contributions and on participants' case studies of practice in their countries.

In Part One, *Citizenship, Equality and Diversity*, we present some of the debates relating to citizenship at the beginning of the twenty-first century, highlighting key issues facing teachers. In chapter one, Audrey Osler examines the growing interest in education for human rights and democracy in the changing global political context. The chapter explores developments in our understandings of education for democratic citizenship, as educators seek to complement education for national citizenship with new approaches which acknowledge the impact of globalisation both on local communities and on nation states. Hugh Starkey further explores the aims of education for democratic citizenship and its relationship to human rights education in chapter two, drawing on a number of key texts, including the UN Convention on the Rights of the Child. He examines language education policies which emphasise equality and diversity and explores ways in which language teachers can put these into practice, building respect for human dignity and equality of rights as the democratic basis for social interaction.

In chapter three, Robin Richardson also examines the concepts of equality and diversity, relating them to identity and, in particular, to representations of Britain and British people. He reports on research undertaken on behalf of the British Council, to discover the degree to which the diversity present in modern day Britain is reflected in activities of the Council. The results of his interviews and questionnaires in Israel and South Africa suggest that if the British Council is to be effective in portraying the values, ideas and achievements of the UK, more attention needs to be given to ethnic and cultural diversity. Richardson highlights a key role for the British Council in promoting debate about the nature of multiculturalism. His findings are particularly pertinent to teachers of English who focus on British cultures. There is a need to challenge institutional bias in management and administration, including arts administration and planning and evaluation processes.

In Part Two, *Teachers Talking Citizenship*, we present case studies from language teachers. In chapter four Kip Cates highlights efforts made by foreign language teachers in Japan to teach for a better world. His is an ambitious agenda, which seeks to translate into practice UNESCO policies on education for peace, democracy and human rights by raising awareness of global issues and developing political literacy through student engagement with social, environmental and economic questions in the language classroom.

Chapter five, which reports on an Argentinean initiative to develop multilingual primary schools, is also concerned with promoting social justice through language learning. Teresa Cañas Davis, the coordinator of the project, explains how in Argentina, effective foreign language education has, until recently been available only to privileged sectors of society. The multilingual primary schools initiative was targeted at young children in the most disadvantaged neighbourhoods in Buenos Aires, including migrants from poorer provinces and from neighbouring States. The project is designed to promote the rights of these children by introducing them to two foreign languages in the early years of schooling. Cañas Davis describes the impact of the project on children, their families and on pedagogy in the project schools. She highlights how project workers have formed partnerships with key organisations, including the British Council, to work to attract the best teachers and resources. This initiative has also had an impact on teacher training institutions, causing them to reflect on their practices.

In chapter six, Vanessa Andreotti challenges language teachers to question the aims and purposes of language teaching, when these aims may be inappropriate to the learners' experiences and contexts. She discusses how, in working as a consultant to a World Bank-funded English language curriculum project in Paraná, Brazil, she invited the group of teachers engaged in the project to reflect on its instrumental purposes. The goal was to prepare students for the job market, yet Andreotti argues there were few, if any, opportunities in the region for students to draw on their linguistic skills. She describes what happened in giving teachers a voice, following her assessment that 'selling the English language as a commodity that would bring status, open the doors of the market and provide higher wages, was like selling an illusion for the vast majority of students'.

Chapter seven is a case study which aims to illustrate some of the changes taking place in English language teaching in Cuban universities, illustrating a move away from a narrow focus on students' future professional contexts to an interdisciplinary, intercultural and humanistic approach. Dolores Corona outlines some of the challenges in encouraging undergraduate students to adopt a more independent project-based approach and, in this case, to focus on the changing role of women in Cuba and the United States.

Chapters eight and nine describe initiatives to promote intercultural learning and an understanding of human rights in two contrasting European contexts. The first case study, by Tuula Penttilä, is an initiative developed in response to increased cultural diversity and to increasing recognition of diversity in Finland. It describes a series of international projects undertaken by one class, studying English, to promote intercultural learning and a sense of global citizenship through the use of communications technology, including video conferencing and the internet. The projects are planned by the teacher, but the specific focus is determined by students' interests and ideas. The second initiative, in Romania, is also a response to changing social conditions and to recognition that education in human rights and democratic citizenship is a critical factor in enabling Romania's transition to full democracy. Margot Brown and Ruxandra Popovici describe the processes of developing *Rights in Deed*, a human rights education textbook designed for schools operating intensive English and bilingual classes. The process included a teacher training programme. The authors argue that the approaches adopted in Romania in education for human rights and democratic citizenship through English language learning might be adapted for students in a range of global contexts.

The final two chapters of the book draw directly from the experiences of the British Council *Language Teaching and Citizenship Education* seminar. In chapter ten Christopher Palmer discusses how task-based learning in the foreign language classroom can enable the thinking skills required for democratic citizenship, sharing ideas that he presented to seminar participants through the example of a maze. Finally, Telma Gimenez reports on the process of including an on-line discussion group for the participants from around the world who wanted to participate in the seminar but were not in a position to travel to Leicestershire, in England. More than 100 messages from these participants were received in the course of the week. These were posted each day, so that those present at the seminar could discuss and respond to the ideas of the remote participants. Gimenez presents their views here and we hope that, together with the contributions of both presenters and participants at the seminar, they will provoke further debate on the role of language learning in teaching for democratic citizenship.

Part One
Citizenship, Equality and Diversity

1

Education for democratic citizenship: new challenges in a globalised world

Audrey Osler

The history of the twentieth century provides us with many examples of individuals who were willing to go to prison, to be exiled from their families and communities, and even to die for democracy and human rights. The names of some, such as Martin Luther King, Nelson Mandela and Aung San Suu Kyi have become symbolic of the struggle of millions of others. Many wars and independence struggles have been fought with the aim of securing democracy and human rights. Yet education planners and policy makers have not always recognised the need to educate young people in democratic practices. Education for democratic citizenship has tended to be low on lists of national education priorities.

At the beginning of the twenty-first century there are signs that things may be changing. Many more national governments are following international organisations such as UNESCO and the Council of Europe in proposing initiatives in human rights and citizenship education. In both new and long established democracies there is a growing emphasis on education for democratic citizenship. Increasingly, it is being acknowledged that education for democracy has a vital contribution in helping secure peace and human rights in the world. There is also a growing recognition that education for national citizenship may be an inadequate response to our changing world, where the processes of globalisation imply increasing global interdependence and greater diversity within local communities. These developments have implications for teachers and for the institutions in which they work, whether these are schools, colleges or universities.

Citizenship is essentially about belonging, about feeling secure and being in a position to exercise one's rights and responsibilities. Education for democratic citizenship therefore needs to address learners' identities and to promote and develop skills for communication and participation. Since these aspects of education are also central to language learning, language teachers are particularly well-placed to make a significant contribution to education for democratic citizenship. Both language learning and learning for democratic citizenship within a globalised world imply openness to the other, respect for diversity and the development of a range of critical skills, including skills of intercultural evaluation. This chapter explores these concepts as they relate to citizenship education. The links between language learning and learning for democratic citizenship are explored in detail in later chapters.

I begin by reviewing the global political context in which policies relating to education for democratic citizenship are being developed. I wish to consider how global developments are posing challenges for citizenship as well as for citizenship education. I address the concept of global education, drawing on research examining global education across four European countries (Osler and Vincent, 2002). I identify some challenges of globalisation for education and consider how education policy-makers are responding to these challenges.

Secondly, I explore the concept of citizenship. What does citizenship mean today? In particular, what does it mean to young people? Citizenship is being introduced or developed as a school subject in countries across the world. I consider whether, in our global age, it is still appropriate or relevant to teach for national citizenship and, if so, how teachers might do this in classrooms where there are children or adults newly-arrived from other parts of the world, who do not hold national citizenship.

Finally, I propose the concept of *cosmopolitan citizenship* as a useful framework for developing new programmes of citizenship education. I will argue that education for cosmopolitan citizenship allows us to address the challenges of globalisation through education while at the same time addressing the needs of learners living in diverse communities. Cosmopolitan citizenship allows us to make the links between the everyday experiences which individuals have within their communities and developments which are taking place at national and global levels (Osler and Starkey, 2003 and 2005a).

A crisis of democracy?

Since the 1980s there have been a number of developments which suggest that the world is becoming more democratic. Between 1980 and 2001, 81 countries took significant steps towards democracy, with 33 military regimes replaced by civilian governments. The number of States holding multi-party elections more than doubled over the period. One hundred and twenty five countries, with 62 per cent of the world population, now have a free press. The number of countries ratifying human rights conventions and covenants has increased dramatically since 1990. The number of countries ratifying the International Covenant on Economic Social and Cultural Rights (ICESCR) and the International Covenant on Civil and Political Rights (ICCPR) grew from 90 to nearly 150 (UNDP, 2002). All but one country has now ratified the UN Convention on the Rights of the Child.

Paradoxically, the start of the twenty-first century also saw a crisis of democracy in States with the longest traditions of democratic governance. The first national elections of the century in the USA, Britain and France were notable for record levels of abstention. The US presidential election in 2000 did not produce an indisputably fair outcome. The 2002 presidential election in France became a referendum on democracy itself, when a candidate of the far right reached the final round.

As we are only too aware, these electoral developments are not the only threats to democracy. The terrorist attacks of 11 September 2001 were launched by activists who, exploiting modern technology, took advantage of the freedoms of movement, of communication and of association in what has been identified as 'an attack on the fundamental principles of freedom, democracy, the rule of law and justice' (Held, 2001). The struggle for human rights and democracy is complex. Many question whether the United States-led military interventions in Afghanistan and Iraq to overthrow authoritarian governments as part of a declared war on terror will, in fact, support the longer-term development of democracy and human rights.

Although trends in world trade, travel and communications have brought us closer together than ever before, the crisis in democracy rests on a feeling among ordinary people that although they can watch what is going on in the world they are unable to change it. Through television or through the internet, they can watch world events evolve, but they feel powerless to influence them.

The Stop the War march held in London in February 2003 attracted over a million participants. The marchers were a very diverse group of people but they had some common agendas. Among the concerns of many of the marchers was the question of whether the overthrow of a dictator and the longer-term struggle for democracy and human rights in Iraq might best be achieved through other means than military force. This protest, and other protests which took place across Britain and across the world on the same day, are an expression of people's horror of war, but they are also much more. They reflect a desire to influence world events and represent a demand that political leaders give consideration to the views of ordinary citizens. Although individuals may feel relatively powerless, they are able to express their views through collective action.

Global education

Education policy makers are searching for appropriate responses to the challenges of globalisation. In a research project undertaken on behalf of the European Commission-funded Network on Global Education in 2001, we examined the different approaches and programmes of *global education* in four European countries: Denmark, England, the Republic of Ireland and the Netherlands (Osler and Vincent, 2002). In order to establish a working definition of global education we drew on definitions from UNESCO and the Council of Europe's North South Centre. Briefly expressed, we identified the aim of global education as follows:

> To build a global culture of peace through the promotion of values, attitudes and behaviour which enable the realisation of democracy, development and human rights.

We defined global education in this way:

> Global education encompasses the strategies, policies and plans that prepare young people and adults for living together in an interdependent world. It is based on the principles of co-operation, non-violence, respect for human rights and cultural diversity, democracy and tolerance. It is characterised by pedagogical approaches based on human rights and a concern for social justice which encourage critical thinking and responsible participation. Learners are encouraged to make links between local, regional and world-wide issues and to address inequality. (Osler and Vincent, 2002: 2)

We were interested in the *strategic approaches* (policies and plans) to global education in each of the four countries. We contend that global education is about *principles* (co-operation, respect for human rights and cultural diversity, democracy); it is about *pedagogical approaches* based on these principles (i.e. critical thinking skills, learner participation). It also addresses specific *knowledge* (an understanding of the current world).

Recognising that the term 'global education' might not be readily used in each of the four countries, we invited our respondents (ministry officials, education workers in voluntary organisations and academics) to comment on official policies and support for a number of educational developments. These included aspects of education which might be considered component parts of global education, including multicultural/ intercultural education, human rights education, global aspects of environmental education and education for sustainable development.

Governments across Europe and internationally have committed themselves to education for international understanding. For example, Ministers of Education, meeting at the 44th session of UNESCO's International Conference on Education in 1994 in Geneva, mindful of their responsibilities in this field, determined:

> to strive resolutely ... to take suitable steps to establish in educational institutions an atmosphere contributing to the success of education for international understanding, so that they become ideal places for the exercise of tolerance, respect for human rights, the practice of democracy and learning about the diversity and wealth of cultural identities. (UNESCO, 1995: 2.2)

Note that UNESCO used the term 'education for international understanding'. Here UNESCO is referring to understanding between nations (the members of UNESCO). Education for international understanding may be part of global education but it cannot be equated with global education. Global education is broader, it encompasses understanding between people. Global education is something in which voluntary or non-governmental organisations (NGOs) play a key role.

In 1995 the General Conference of UNESCO approved an *Integrated Framework of Action on Education for Peace, Human Rights and Democracy* at its 28th session in Paris, which identified policies and actions to be taken at institutional, national and international levels to realise such education. It states:

> There must be education for peace, human rights and democracy. It cannot, however, be restricted to specialised subjects and knowledge. The whole of education must transmit this message and the atmosphere of the institution must be in harmony with the application of democratic standards. (UNESCO: 1995: IV. 17)

It is this education for *peace, human rights and democracy* that is global education. The intention is that education for peace, human rights and democracy should be a mainstream concern and part of the entitlement of every learner. The UNESCO General Conference recognised that any attempt to incorporate these issues into the curriculum will need to be matched by processes of democratisation within education authorities and schools.

Global education and democracy in schools

The UNESCO statement echoes the sentiment of the Council of Europe Committee of Ministers' Recommendation some ten years earlier, on teaching and learning about human rights:

> Democracy is best learned in a democratic setting where participation is encouraged, where views can be expressed openly and discussed, where there is freedom of expression for pupils and teachers, and where there is fairness and justice. An appropriate climate is, therefore, an essential complement to effective learning about human rights. (Council of Europe, 1985, re-printed in Osler and Starkey, l996)

I am arguing that global education is necessarily education for democracy. For education in democracy to be effective, the institution of the school must be developed in a democratic way, guaranteeing the right of children and young people to form views and 'to express those views freely in all matters affecting [them]' and to have those views 'taken seriously in accordance with [their] age and maturity' in line with Article 12 of the UN Convention on the Rights of the Child 1989 (CRC). Nevertheless, policy statements are likely to remain at the level of exhortation, unless opportunities are created for national policy-makers, education authorities, schools and teachers to explore the meanings of these documents in depth and devise action strategies at each level through to the classroom. It is only when such democratic processes are set up that education for peace, democracy and human rights will be mainstreamed. Pedagogical approaches based on human rights require teachers to have an understanding of children's rights. One starting point is to assess the degree to which current school policies and practices are in conformity with the CRC. Drawing on the CRC, we have developed an instrument which is designed to enable teachers (and students) to evaluate the degree to which their school supports children's rights (see Osler and Starkey, 2005a).

One way in which schools can apply the principle of democracy and promote student participation is through the engagement of students in school boards and school councils. In Denmark legal provision is made for two student representatives to sit alongside two teacher representatives on these school boards, where parents have a very powerful voice and make up the majority representatives. In the Netherlands there is a statutory obligation for each school to have a 'participation council'. At secondary level this includes equal numbers of teacher and either parent or student representatives. A number of Irish schools have had school councils for some time. In Ireland, the Education Act 1998 provides for the setting up of school councils and for the more democratic engagement of students in the running of schools. The school board is obliged to give support to an existing school council and to assist students in establishing a school council where they wish to do so. Both Germany and Sweden have also made legal provision for the democratic representation of students in school decision-making (Davies and Kirkpatrick, 2000).

England was the only one of our case study countries currently without statutory support for student participation in decision-making. Around one in three primary schools and two in three secondary schools now have a school council. Yet only one in ten operates with real effectiveness, according to Schools Council UK. Research suggests that ineffective school councils can be counter-productive, causing students to become disillusioned with democratic practices and disaffected (Cunningham, 2000; Osler, 2000b). There is evidence from a wide range of countries across the world that disaffection, disillusionment and denial of student voice may lead to increased levels of violence (Harber, 2004; Osler and Starkey, 2005b).

Global education and education policy

Of course, it is possible to promote co-operation, democratic approaches and responsible participation without necessarily encouraging learners to make links between local, regional and world-wide issues. Education systems are responding to the processes of globalisation in a number of diverse ways. In each of the four case study countries global education is recognised as being of importance and is supported by broad policy statements at central government level. Each country acknowledges the need to educate its citizens to live together in an interdependent world and makes provision for some form of social and political education, whether or not the term citizenship education is used.

Generally speaking, ministries of education recognise the importance of some form of global education, particularly within the compulsory years of schooling. They acknowledge, either implicitly or explicitly, the economic effects of globalisation and the importance of economic competitiveness within this context. In the UK, a key Government response to the processes of globalisation is the determination to raise standards of achievement in education, so that learners will have the skills to compete successfully in a world job market. The 2001 White Paper on Education, *Schools Achieving Success*, placed emphasis on the basic skills of literacy and numeracy:

A generation ago Britain tolerated an education system with a long tail of poor achievement because there was a plentiful supply of unskilled and semi-skilled jobs. This is no longer the case. By breaking the cycle of underachievement in education we can extend opportunity across society.

To prosper in the 21st century competitive global economy, Britain must transform the knowledge and skills of its population. Every child, whatever their circumstances, requires an education that equips them for work and prepares them to succeed in the wider economy and in society. (DfES, 2001: 5. 1.1 and 1.2)

The UK White Paper stressed accountability, inspection, meeting the needs of the individual, consumer choice and improved incentives for teacher per-formance as means by which educational standards can be raised in this global competition. It made no reference to cultural diversity, nor to the com-munity learning and experiences of citizenship which young people bring to school (Osler and Starkey, 2001, 2002b and 2003). The emphasis on com-petition rather than on co-operation at a global level translates into policies at a local level which require schools and learners to compete in order to achieve higher standards.

Competition is stressed at the expense of co-operation. Young people are ex-pected to learn 'how to reason, think logically and creatively and take in-creasing responsibility for their own learning' (DfES, 2001: 18. 3.2). For young people to take responsibility for their own learning implies that they will be consulted. In other words we might expect that at school level students will be guaranteed access to a forum where they can express their views and that they can engage in the processes of school decision-making, either directly or through a representative system. For young people to be able to take responsibility implies the democratisation of schools. There are, however, to date, no legislative proposals in England which address student participation or representation in school decision-making. The accountability of schools and education authorities does not appear to extend to learners who, though responsible for their own learning, are not guaranteed involve-ment in school governance or in decision-making relating to the curriculum. There is no legislation in England to ensure that young people are routinely consulted about matters or procedures affecting them in schools, in line with the State's obligations under Article 12 of the UN Convention on the Rights of the Child. Nor are there any processes for student appeal if an individual believes they have experienced an injustice. The model of school effective-ness being promoted is not underpinned by democratic values.

These understandings of school effectiveness are not, by any means, peculiar or exclusive to the UK. For some years now, one response to the forces of globalisation has been for governments of industrialised countries to place greater emphasis on the need for education systems to respond to the need for international competitiveness, rather than to emphasise the need for greater international understanding. The pressure on schools is therefore to improve standards so that students will be well placed to make their contribution to an internationally competitive workforce. Globalisation is seen largely as an economic process and not as a potential force for greater democratisation. The need for greater democratisation in education as a means of shaping and influencing the ongoing processes of globalisation is overlooked. The focus is in economic competitiveness, not on global co-operation. From this perspective, education for peace, human rights and democracy is unlikely to be widely recognised as a mainstream issue. It is unlikely to be addressed as a priority in the day-to-day management of schools or to feature on the agenda of headteachers' management training.

In 1998 the report of the government advisory group on education for citizenship and democracy in schools in England was published (QCA, 1998). This report, known as the Crick report after the group's Chair, Bernard Crick, gives relatively little attention either to the global dimension of citizenship or to ways in which schools might promote and strengthen democracy (Osler, 2000a, Osler and Starkey 2002a). Although governments in a range of industrialised countries, including a number of western European countries and Japan, recognise a role for global education, it is rarely a funding priority within ministries of education. It is normally the ministry of foreign affairs/international development which takes a lead in supporting educational initiatives to promote international development and solidarity with the poorest countries of the world. While such programmes may explore questions of global interdependence, they are less likely to tackle questions of human rights and social justice at home.

Citizenship in a global age
Glenys Kinnock argues that the chief task of citizens is:

> To globalise social progress. There needs to be a response to the aspirations of people everywhere for decent and productive jobs in conditions of freedom, equality, security and human dignity. As citizens, we have a responsibility to inform ourselves and press for greater understanding of the nature of development, and the need for growth with equality. That means understanding complex issues, but the effective campaigns against debt, and for arms control, prove that

this is not an impediment to progress. These campaigns prove that people will grapple with a lot of technical detail if they believe that there is an important case to be made. Armed with the right information, committed citizens believe that they have influence, and that they can change the world. Whether it is a sponsored bike ride for Nicaragua, or lighting a candle for peace, or running a marathon for Mozambique, many of us work in different ways to open people's eyes, ears and hearts.

She goes on to make the links between national and international concerns:

Perversely, developed societies – like our own – appear to be under growing pressure to look inwards. The shaving of overseas aid budgets in several industrialised countries in recent years is just one symptom of this widespread rejection of an international perspective – although targets have now been set by many countries to reverse this trend. Such a blinkered view is not only a matter of moral regret, it is dangerously myopic in an age in which the fortunes, and misfortunes, of nations are more intimately linked than ever before. Common sense alone tells us that some issues are of such diversity and dimension that they simply cannot be dealt with by governments acting alone, or even several governments acting in concert. ... We need to understand that dealing with national issues of fairness, equality and liberty also requires, by necessity, that we look outwards. (Kinnock, 2002: xiii)

In these two statements Glenys Kinnock is examining the practice of citizenship. Citizenship involves solidarity with others and engagement in campaigning activities. Citizenship is also about engaging with others and seeking to influence others. It is about beliefs and attitudes and about making a difference.

Citizenship as feeling, status and practice

Citizenship is most often understood as a *status*. The legal status of citizen is currently determined as relating to a particular nation state. Political debates and policy developments focus on who is, and who is not, a citizen, with particular rights and obligations. In this sense citizenship is exclusive, since there is a clear-cut distinction between those who have this status and those who do not. Yet citizenship is much more than status, it also involves *feeling*, the degree to which individuals feel they belong, and citizen participation and engagement, what can be termed the *practice* of citizenship. I will consider citizenship as status, feeling and practice.

Citizenship as status

The rights most regularly associated with citizenship are those to live and work in a particular country and to vote. The State protects citizens through laws and policing. It provides some collective benefits such as education, health care, and transport infrastructure. In return, citizens contribute to the costs of collective benefits through taxation.

Whereas in France the subjects of an absolute monarch received the status of citizen through the 1789 revolution and the word citizen has very positive connotations associated with freedom, equality and solidarity, in Britain people are far less confident about their legal status as citizens. The concept of British subject has lingered throughout the twentieth century. The status of citizen was first created by statute in 1948 with the introduction of the 'citizen of the United Kingdom and colonies'. It is primarily through changes in immigration policy, and through a desire to distinguish between British subjects living in the UK and those in Commonwealth countries who were eventually denied free access to Britain, that a distinction was made between British subjects and British citizens. The term 'British citizen' was first introduced under the Immigration Act 1981 as a means to exclude Commonwealth citizens from freely entering the UK. It is not perhaps surprising that the term citizen neither resonates positively nor is clearly understood, since the legal concept is somewhat muddled. While citizenship has been developed to exclude, certain voting rights are not exclusive to British citizens:

> Since the rights and responsibilities of British citizenship are not restricted to British nationals, the legal concept is not clearly defined. For example, Commonwealth and Irish citizens resident in the Untied Kingdom enjoy voting rights in local and national elections. (Smith, 1997: xi)

Although the struggle for democracy and citizenship is an ongoing one, in the sense that the full realisation of civil, political and social rights for all has yet to be achieved, in Britain the status of citizen is not something which has been struggled for. There is not a positive identification of citizenship with nationality. Indeed, nationalism and the link between citizenship and nationality is used by many political groups to exclude. It is therefore inevitable that the content of the school subject citizenship is likely to be controversial. By conceiving citizenship as a universal, based on universal human rights, there is an opportunity to explore citizenship in a more inclusive way.

Citizenship as feeling

Whether or not individuals have the status of citizen, the degree to which they identify with a particular State may vary. Although governments and communities and the media may promote feelings of national identity through national holidays, sporting events, jubilees, parades and public service broadcasting, individuals are likely to vary in the degree to which they feel they are part of the nation.

Although democratic states aspire to treat all citizens alike on the basis of equality, individuals and groups may have difficulties in accessing those services. So, for example, parents of children with special educational needs report difficulties in securing their child's right to education. Other groups may access services but not on the basis of equality. For example, black community groups in Britain express concern at the differentials in achievement between different groupings of children. Overall, 48 per cent of students aged 16 years gained 5 or more A* to C GCSE grades in 2000, but students of Caribbean heritage were well below this, with just 27 per cent achieving these exam grades nationally (Tikly *et al.*, 2002). If individuals are not accessing services on the basis of equality, or they feel they are not doing so, they are likely to feel excluded. The sense of belonging, which is a prerequisite of participative citizenship, is missing.

For many citizens, it may be easier to identify with a particular place or region. An individual may declare: 'I feel at home in Birmingham' or 'I feel proud to come from Yorkshire'. Our research in the multicultural city of Leicester, with young people aged 10 to 18 years, sought to establish ways in which they understood and identified with various communities (Osler and Starkey, 2003). We gave each individual a disposable camera and invited them to make them an exhibition of photographs with captions. Their captions and commentaries show how many of them identified with a particular religious community. This was not generally an exclusive identification; the young people were also conscious of diversity and saw it as a very positive aspect of their city and locality:

> I am Hindu, born in Leicester and proud of being a Hindu.

> I'm Asian and my religion is Islam. I live in a multicultural area with Christians, Sikhs, Muslims and Hindus.

> My street is ... in Highfields, there are many people living there, people of many cultures, religion and race. I like my street people and these many cultures which are fascinating and you can learn more in life with many cultures surrounding you.

Most commonly they identified with their city or neighbourhood or with other places, particularly public spaces such as parks, schools, shopping centres and libraries where they could access particular facilities and meet friends:

> My church is a very important place for me. I am not very religious but I love going to pray every Sunday. It's a really old building and on its other side there is our community centre. At my community centre is where people go and relax and chill. At the same centre there are clubs, karate, drama etc. I do karate at this centre and it is good fun.

> All my childhood memories! [I] played in this park with all my cousins and friends. This park is very important to me as it is my childhood.

> This is the famous Belgrave Road. It represents my community. It has many Indian retailer shops ... In Belgrave Road there are a library, leisure area, local park. Many tourists from other cities visit Belgrave Road to do some shopping.

Citizenship as a feeling is often considered to be a question of identity and for these young people many of their multiple identities are situated in their local communities (Osler and Starkey, 2003). For these young people, as for many others across the world, the local community remains a key locus of identity. As Legrain (2002: 9) notes, both identity and 'democracy [remain] rooted in local communities and nation states'.

Our research with young people supports the notion that identity and citizenship as feeling may frequently be situated in local communities and, to a greater or lesser extent in one or more nation states. Yet many people, who have the status of British citizen, do not find it easy to identify with the nation or with national symbols. We have noted reluctance among teachers and student teachers to endorse the use of national symbols, such as the flag, in school contexts. For many, such symbols may be tainted with uncritical patriotism, discredited imperialism or an exclusive nationalism.

Some citizens who seek to belong may nevertheless be excluded. In the 1960s E. R. Braithwaite, the author of the novel *To Sir, With Love*, summed up the kinds of contradictions which a citizen may feel:

> In spite of my years of residence in Britain, any service I might render the community in times of war or peace, any contribution I might make or wish to make, or any feeling I might entertain towards Britain and the British, I – like all other colored persons in Britain – am considered an 'immigrant'. Although this term indicates that we have secured entry into Britain, it describes a continuing condition in which we have

> no real hope of ever enjoying the desired transition to full responsible citizenship. (Braithwaite, 1967, quoted in Fryer, 1984: 382)

Braithwaite reminds us that for some citizens, even the choice to identify with the nation can be denied. Citizenship as feeling is often considered to be a question of identity. But the choice to identify with a particular group can be denied by an excluding society. Braithwaite's observation, that 'full responsible citizenship' was denied black settlers, still has some resonance today for particular groups. Many British citizens continue today to be viewed by many as outsiders, as can be observed in more recent debates about the allegiance of British Muslims (Richardson, 1997 and 2004; Jawad and Benn, 2003).

Formal and informal barriers to full citizenship on the basis of gender and/or ethnicity continue to exist in many societies. They have been well documented in the case of the USA:

> Becoming citizens of the [American] commonwealth has been much more difficult for ethnic groups of color and for women from all racial, ethnic and cultural groups than for mainstream males. Groups of color have experienced three major problems in becoming citizens of the United States. First, they were denied citizenship by laws. Second, when legal barriers to citizenship were eliminated, they were often denied educational experiences that would enable them to attain the cultural and language characteristics needed to function effectively in the mainstream society. Third, they were often denied the opportunity to fully participate in mainstream society even when they attained these characteristics because of ... discrimination. (Banks, 1997: xi)

Citizenship as practice

The young people who took part in our research project in Leicester have a strong sense of solidarity with others in their neighbourhoods and with people in other parts of the world. We found that they are more likely to engage in campaigning activities or fund-raising activities than get involved in formal politics. These kinds of activities, whether related to a local issue, such as a threatened school closure; an international emergency, such as a flood in India; or an international issue, such as the Palestinian cause, are the kind of activities in which they feel they can make a difference.

The liberal tradition of citizenship stresses the rights of citizens. Universal human rights are universal entitlements, in the sense that they can be claimed by all. The Universal Declaration of Human Rights 1948 (UDHR) defined and codified these rights, addressing civil, political and social rights. Rights are guaranteed through legal frameworks, usually, but not exclusively, at national level. The other major tradition of citizenship is the civic republican tradition, which stresses the obligations of citizens to participate by being prepared to stand for office and by undertaking service to the State. Although these two traditions are often seen as being in tension, efforts have been made to establish a coherent synthesis. Ruth Lister suggests that citizenship needs to be understood as a status and as *practice*:

> My starting point has been to reformulate and bring together the two great historical traditions of citizenship, those of civic republicanism and liberal rights, in a *critical synthesis*. Citizenship is thereby understood as both a *status*, carrying a set of rights including social and reproductive rights, and as a *practice*, involving political practice broadly defined so as to include the kind of informal politics in which women are more likely to engage. The relationship is a dynamic one and one which is fired by the notion of *human agency*. My interoperation of the two traditions has been informed by the principle of *inclusiveness*. More broadly, this principle involves strengthening the inclusive side of citizenship's coin while explicitly acknowledging, and as far as possible challenging, its exclusionary side both within and at the borders of nation-states. In the latter case, this means that a feminist reconstruction of citizenship has to be *internationalist* and *multi-layered* in its thinking. It is only through such a perspective that we can address the limitations of citizenship which are thrown into relief in the face of growing numbers of migrants and asylum seekers and of a nation-state under pressure from within and without. (Lister, 1997: 196)

Building on Lister's conception of an inclusive citizenship, we have proposed a recognition of citizenship as not simply status and practice, but also as feeling (Osler and Starkey, 2005a). We need an inclusive approach to citizenship but one which also acknowledges the feelings of individuals, and their multiple identities. Participative citizenship necessarily requires a sense of belonging. This is especially important when considering citizenship education. Without the affective dimension, it is unlikely we will engage learners.

The inclusive side of citizenship refers to universal human rights. All are included in this definition of a community of citizens. As I have sought to demonstrate, it is not only national boundaries but other factors, linked to gender, class and ethnicity, which can serve to exclude. An internationalist and multi-layered perspective requires individuals not only to concern themselves with the quality of life within their own national boundaries, but also with human rights concerns elsewhere in the world. Pressure on national

governments is a means by which individuals and groups can bring pressure
to bear on the international community:

> Our national citizenship and our national government are important to
> us chiefly to the degree that they become the instruments by which we
> exert our influence in the international community of nations. (Ignatieff,
> 1995: 76)

Cosmopolitan citizenship

I conclude by proposing the concept of cosmopolitan citizenship as a useful
one for global educators. We have seen that although governments have
sought to respond to globalisation through policy development, global education has not yet been mainstreamed within schools. Effective mainstreaming
is likely to require *both* a specific curriculum space and permeation of the
whole school curriculum and ethos.

A number of political theorists argue that we need to re-think democracy in
the context of our increasingly interdependent world. David Held (1995 and
1996) proposes a model of 'cosmopolitan democracy', challenging the
notion that the nation state is the most appropriate locus for democracy. He
argues for the building of human rights into the constitution of States and for
the creation and development of regional and global institutions, which
would coexist alongside States, but over-ride them on those issues which
escape their control, such as monetary management, environmental questions, elements of security and new forms of communication. Indeed, many
such reforms have been introduced since the mid-1990s. For example, in the
UK, the Human Rights Act 1998 incorporates the European Convention on
Human Rights into domestic law.

The terrorist attacks of 11 September 2001 have brought these concerns into
sharper focus. Governments and intergovernmental organisations are required to re-think their global responsibilities, and work co-operatively and
with moral consistency with regard to human rights, justice and aid. Indeed,
it can be argued that for wealthy countries such policies are in their self-
interest. Beck (2001), in a response to the events of 11 September 2001,
stresses that cosmopolitan democracy involves solidarity and respect for difference within communities and States as well as at a global level:

> What are we fighting for when we fight against global terrorism? My
> answer is that we should fight for the right to be cosmopolitan, which
> is fundamentally based on the recognition of the otherness of others. ...
> Cosmopolitan states emphasise the necessity for solidarity with
> foreigners both inside and outside the national borders ... [they] strug-

gle not only against terror, but against the causes of terror. ...they do this by seeking the solution of global problems ... which cannot be solved by individual nations on their own. (Beck, 2001: 34).

Education for cosmopolitan citizenship is a route through which we may realise global education. It will involve young people in exploring the status, feelings and practice of citizenship. It will involve teachers in making explicit the connections between local, national and global concerns.

Globalisation and increased interdependence now mean that organisations, people and events over which we may have little influence affect our everyday lives. The terrorist attacks of 11 September 2001 and their on-going consequences have made it impossible to avoid this reality. Preparing young people to participate as cosmopolitan citizens, capable of shaping the future of their own communities and of engaging in democratic processes at all levels, has become an urgent task. The nation state is longer the only locus for democracy. The challenge is to develop democratic processes at all levels from the global to the local. At the same time, individuals practise citizenship within local contexts. Whether engaged in democratic processes at local, national or international levels, citizens need skills that will enable them to participate and live together in contexts of diversity.

Learners will require skills and attitudes which allow them to make connections between different contexts and situations, and to respond to constant change. Not only will learners need to apply this in schools and in local communities and to understand national, regional and international contexts, they will also have to be able to make connections between these contexts. The greatest challenge that cosmopolitan citizens face is being able to make connections, to critique and to evaluate within contexts of cultural diversity.

Education for cosmopolitan citizenship also implies a broader understanding of national identity; it requires recognition that British identity, for example, may be experienced differently by different people. It also implies recognition of our common humanity and a sense of solidarity with others. It is insufficient, however, to feel and express a sense of solidarity with others elsewhere, if we cannot establish a sense of solidarity with others in our own communities, especially those others whom we perceive to be different from ourselves. The challenge is to accept shared responsibility for our common future and for solving our common problems.

How then can we educate cosmopolitan citizens so that they are able to recognise our common humanity, make connections between their own lives and those of others, operating in contexts of cultural diversity and change?

Cosmopolitan citizens need to acquire the skills of intercultural evaluation (Hall, 2000; Parekh, 2000). Human rights provide us with a set of internationally agreed principles, as formulated in such internationally agreed texts as the Universal Declaration of Human Rights (UDHR) and the UN Convention on the Rights of the Child (CRC), against which we can make critical assessments.

Such texts provide us with a framework from which a school or any other learning community can derive a set of explicit, shared democratic values. These texts provide us with a set of principles against which we can critically reflect on our own culture, values, beliefs and behaviours and those of our fellow citizens. From such a reference point it becomes possible to respect others and their cultures, while not necessarily accepting all aspects of another culture:

> Citizenship in a plural society implies a security in one's own culture – but not an unquestioning security. It also implies a critical respect for the culture, beliefs and values of the other even in their difference, a critical respect for difference. Rational dialogue (that is, meaningful exchange of views, not monologue, nor command, nor wilful, blind or spiteful discourse) between the different parties is essential, so that all may equitably contribute to the decisions taken and the judgements made. (Figueroa, 2000: 57)

Human rights do not provide a set of clear-cut rules, but general principles. It is therefore possible to recognise that these principles might be secured and upheld within a variety of cultural contexts, by different means. Language teachers are already encouraging their students to reflect on their own cultures, values, beliefs and behaviours as they learn about the cultures, values, beliefs and behaviours of the people whose language they are studying. In this way they are developing skills of intercultural communication (Byram *et al.*, 2002; Starkey, 2002 and 2005; Willems, 2002). The challenge that language teachers face is to build upon this learning and support students in developing skills of intercultural evaluation.

Learning communities built on human rights principles, which uphold rights in education, also provide a model of human rights and democracy and the experience of human rights. Education for cosmopolitan citizenship, founded on human rights, will enable learners to recognise our common humanity and provide a sense of belonging to a global community. Good language teachers must necessarily be cosmopolitan citizens. The languages classroom is a key place in which the knowledge, skills and attitudes necessary for cosmopolitan citizenship can be developed and practised. Learners will need opportunities to express solidarity with those whose rights are infringed; opportunities to exercise their rights to participation; and the skills to do this within contexts of cultural diversity. Although the language classroom does not exist in isolation, it can be developed as a model of democratic practice. The participative learning styles which characterise good practice in language teaching and learning are also those which support education for democratic citizenship.

References

Banks, J. (1997) *Educating Citizens in a Multicultural Society*. New York: Teachers College Press.

Beck, U. (2001) The fight for a cosmopolitan future, *New Statesman*, 5 November: 33-34.

Byram, M., Gribkova, B. and Starkey, H. (2002) *Developing the Intercultural Dimension in Language Teaching*. Strasbourg: Council of Europe Language Policy Division.

Cunningham, J. (2000) Democratic practice in a secondary school, in A. Osler (Ed.) *Citizenship and Democracy in Schools: diversity, identity, equality*. Stoke-on-Trent: Trentham.

Davies, L. and Kirkpatrick, G. (2000) *The Eurodem Project: a review of pupil democracy in Europe*. London: Children's Rights Alliance.

Department for Education and Skills (DfES) (2001) *Schools Achieving Success*. White Paper. London: DfES. www.dfes.gov.uk/achievingsuccess

Figueroa, P. (2000) Citizenship education for a plural society, in A. Osler (Ed.) *Citizenship and Democracy in Schools: diversity, identity, equality*. Stoke-on-Trent: Trentham.

Fryer, P. (1984) *Staying Power: the history of black people in Britain*. London: Pluto Press.

Hall, S. (2000) Multicultural citizens: monocultural citizenship, in: N. Pearce and J. Hallgarten (eds.) *Tomorrow's Citizens: critical debates in citizenship and education*. London: Institute for Public Policy Research.

Harber, C. (2004) *Schooling as Violence: how schools harm pupils and societies*. London: RoutledgeFalmer.

Held, D. (1995) Democracy and the new international order, in D. Archibugi and D. Held (eds.) *Cosmopolitan Democracy*. Cambridge: Polity Press.

Held, D. (1996) *Models of Democracy*. 2nd edition. Cambridge: Polity Press.

Held, D. (2001) *Violence and Justice in a Global Age*, 14 September. www.opendemocracy.net

Ignatieff, M. (1995) *Blood and Belonging*. London: Viking Press.

Jawad, H. and Benn, T. (2003) (eds.) *Muslim Women in the United Kingdom and Beyond: experiences and images*. Leiden: Brill.

Kinnock, G. (2002) Foreword, in: A. Osler and K. Vincent *Citizenship and the Challenge of Global Education*. Stoke-on Trent: Trentham.

Legrain, P. (2002) *Open World: the truth about globalisation*. London: Abacus.

Lister, R. (1997) *Citizenship: feminist perspectives*. London: Macmillan.

Osler, A. (2000a) The Crick Report: difference, equality and racial justice, *Curriculum Journal*, 11 (1) 25-37.

Osler, A. (2000b) Children's rights, responsibilities and understandings of school discipline, *Research Papers in Education* 15 (1): 49-67.

Osler, A. and Starkey, H. (1996) *Teacher Education and Human Rights*. London: David Fulton.

Osler, A. and Starkey, H. (1998) Children's rights and citizenship: some implications for the management of schools, *International Journal of Children's Rights* 6: 313-333.

Osler, A. and Starkey, H. (2001) Young People in Leicester (UK): community, identity and citizenship, *Interdialogos* 2 (01): 48-49.

Osler, A., and Starkey, H. (2002a) Education for Citizenship: mainstreaming the fight against racism? *European Journal of Education*, 37 (2): 143-159.

Osler, A. and Starkey, H. (2002b) Young people as cosmopolitan citizens, in F. Audigier and N. Bottani (eds.) *Learning to Live Together and Curricular Content.* Geneva: International Bureau of Education.

Osler, A. and Starkey, H. (2003) Learning for cosmopolitan citizenship: theoretical debates and young people's experiences, *Educational Review* 55 (3): 243-254.

Osler, A. and Starkey, H. (2005a) *Changing Citizenship: democracy and inclusion in education.* Buckingham: Open University Press.

Osler, A. and Starkey, H. (2005b) Violence in schools and representations of young people: a critique of government policies in France and England, *Oxford Review of Education* 31 (2).

Osler, A. and Vincent, K. (2002) *Citizenship and the Challenge of Global Education.* Stoke-on-Trent: Trentham.

Parekh, B. (2000) *Rethinking Multiculturalism: cultural diversity and political theory.* London: Macmillan.

Qualifications and Curriculum Authority (QCA) (1998) *Education for Citizenship and the Teaching of Democracy in Schools* (The Crick Report). London: QCA.

Richardson, R. (1997) *Islamophobia: a challenge for us all.* London: Runnymede Trust.

Richardson, R. (ed.) (2004) *Islamophobia: issues, challenges and action.* Stoke-on-Trent: Trentham with the Uniting Britain Trust, London.

Smith, T. (1997) Preface, in: J. P.Gardner (ed.) *Citizenship: the White Paper.* London: British Institute of International and Comparative Law.

Starkey, H. (2002) *Democratic Citizenship, Languages, Diversity and Human Rights.* Strasbourg: Council of Europe Language Policy Division.

Starkey, H. (2005) Language teaching for democratic citizenship, in: A. Osler and H. Starkey (eds.) *Citizenship and Language Learning: international perspectives.* Stoke-on-Trent: Trentham.

Tikly, L. Osler, A. and Hill, J. (2002) *Ethnic Minority Achievement Grant: analysis of LEA action plans.* London: Department of Education and Skills.

United Nations Development Programme (UNDP) (2002) *Human Development Report 2002: deepening democracy in a fragmented world.* Oxford: Oxford University Press.

United Nations Educational Scientific and Cultural Organisation (UNESCO) (1995) *Declaration and Integrated Framework of Action on Education for Peace, Human Rights and Democracy.* Paris UNESCO.

Willems, G.M. (2002) *Language Teacher Education Policy Promoting Linguistic Diversity and Intercultural Communication.* Strasbourg: Council of Europe Language Policy Division.

2

Language teaching for democratic citizenship

Hugh Starkey

Education for citizenship and the promotion of language learning for intercultural communication are both responses to the political and social realities of globalisation. Global migration, both of specialised labour and of individuals and groups displaced by war, political instability or dire economic conditions, has produced cosmopolitan societies across the world. Simultaneously, political movements based on ethnic, religious and narrowly nationalist ideologies threaten democracy and challenge existing political and social structures. In this context, education in general and education for citizenship in particular, provide the mechanism for transmitting those core shared values that are essential if just and peaceful democratic societies are to be developed. Language education is increasingly construed as contributing to citizenship education. The aims and purposes of language teaching and learning, in many contexts, support education for democratic citizenship.

As Audrey Osler notes (this volume), there are increasing numbers of States that may be considered to be liberal democracies. In these countries, human rights are generally respected and fundamental freedoms promoted. Governments may be replaced periodically following free and fair elections. Nonetheless, even in the most proudly democratic societies, significant inequalities remain, sections of the population may be marginalised and antidemocratic forces misuse freedom of speech to promote xenophobia and nationalistic populism.

Democracy, even where it is long established, is a potentially fragile system. The openness and freedoms that are the essence of a democratic way of life also provide scope for non-democratic groups, including those resorting to terrorism, to organise and actively seek to destabilise and ultimately discredit and overthrow elected authorities. By definition, democracy requires the commitment of ordinary people and this is only achieved where the people understand both the characteristics of a democratic way of life and the consequences of its potential loss. Education is crucial to achieving a culture of democracy.

Increasingly, governments are putting in place specific school programmes of education for democratic citizenship. Examples can be found throughout the world (Torney-Purta *et al*. 1999; Davies, 2000b). This chapter examines the aims and purposes of citizenship education as they have been developed by the Council of Europe at a regional level and promoted at global level by the British Council. It then examines the ways in which language education policies developed in a European context are also designed to promote and reinforce democracy. It identifies a number of challenges faced by language teachers and proposes some practical responses. It concludes by suggesting the importance of recognising and welcoming the potentially significant contributions of language learning to citizenship and democracy, which are themselves elements of a just and peaceful world order.

Aims and purposes of education for democratic citizenship

There is general agreement across governments of all political persuasions in Europe as to what constitutes Education for Democratic Citizenship (EDC) and its aims and purposes. The ministers of education of all Council of Europe Member States periodically make recommendations to their governments on priority issues for education policy. These recommendations also summarise and synthesise the research and development studies that contribute to policy formation. In 2002 the Committee of Ministers of the Council of Europe, representing over 40 Member States, recommended that European governments: 'make education for democratic citizenship a priority objective of educational policy-making and reforms' (Council of Europe, 2002: 2).

The reasons for this recommendation are twofold. The first is that the mission and purpose of the Council of Europe is to promote justice and peace in the region through a strengthening of democracy and human rights. This mission parallels, at European level, the purposes of the global organisation that is the United Nations and its constituent bodies such as UNESCO. The second is that certain trends in European society are causing concern as running counter to this first, peaceful objective.

The relationship of EDC to the overall mission of the Council of Europe is recalled in the Recommendation as follows:

> education for democratic citizenship is fundamental to the Council of Europe's primary task of promoting a free, tolerant and just society, and [that] it contributes, alongside the Organisation's other activities, to defending the values and principles of freedom, pluralism, human rights and the rule of law, which are the foundations of democracy;
> (Council of Europe, 2002: 2)

In other words, the collective vision of the Member States of the Council of Europe is of societies that are 'free, tolerant and just'. Such societies can only be established on the basis of democracy, and this in turn implies 'freedom, pluralism, human rights and the rule of law'. Education contributes to fulfilling this vision by enabling citizens to understand the meaning and the implications of democracy and human rights. It is an important element of a democratic society, but it also depends on laws that are made and enforced at national level. In particular Member States are expected to have in place effective legislation to promote equality of rights and outlaw inappropriate discrimination.

This vision, and the institutions, including educational and legal frameworks, that have been put in place at European, national and local levels to support it, derive from the founding instruments of the Council of Europe. These are the Statute (1949) and the European Convention for the Protection of Human Rights and Fundamental Freedoms (ECHR) (1950). Both these instruments refer explicitly to the United Nations. They enact and strengthen, at European level, values and standards that are universal. This too, is explicitly re-affirmed in the Recommendation:

> Recalling the primacy of the Convention for the Protection of Human Rights and Fundamental Freedoms and the other Council of Europe and United Nations instruments in guaranteeing to individuals the capacity to exercise their inalienable rights in a democratic society.
> (Council of Europe, 2002: 1)

Human rights education is thus an essential component of EDC. Citizens may be defined as those able to exercise their rights and responsibilities in a democratic society and in order to exercise their rights they must be familiar with them and understand the scope and the limitations of their rights. This is recognised in the Recommendation, which notes that: 'For instance, it

[EDC] might involve civic, political or human rights education, all of which contribute to education for democratic citizenship without covering it completely' (Council of Europe, 2002: 3).

From one perspective EDC contributes positively to the construction of a free, tolerant and peaceful world. The other perspective, acknowledged by the European ministers of education, is the need to act defensively to protect the hard won but still fragile achievements of democratic institutions based on human rights from those forces that may undermine them. The Recommendation asserts that governments are:

> Concerned by the growing levels of political and civic apathy and lack of confidence in democratic institutions, and by the increased cases of corruption, racism, xenophobia, aggressive nationalism, intolerance of minorities, discrimination and social exclusion, all of which are major threats to the security, stability and growth of democratic societies. (Council of Europe, 2002: 1)

These concerns seek to confront, on the one hand, apathy and lack of trust in democracy and, on the other, failures of democratic systems (corruption, racism, discrimination and social exclusion) and anti-democratic political forces, particularly those promoting 'xenophobia, aggressive nationalism, intolerance of minorities'. Apathy and lack of trust can only be addressed by confronting the failure of democracy to deliver justice (for instance through political education) and by positively promoting a culture of human rights (for instance by stressing the importance of antiracism). This is also clearly expressed in the Recommendation, in which ministers advocate:

> ■ combining the acquisition of knowledge, attitudes and skills, and giving priority to those which reflect the fundamental values to which the Council of Europe is particularly attached, notably human rights and the rule of law;
>
> ■ paying particular attention to the acquisition of the attitudes necessary for life in multicultural societies, which respect differences and are concerned with their environment, which is undergoing rapid and often unforeseeable changes.

> To that end, it would be appropriate to implement educational approaches and teaching methods which aim at learning to live together in a democratic society, and at combating aggressive nationalism, racism and intolerance and eliminate violence and extremist thinking and behaviour. (Council of Europe, 2002: 3)

The goals of promoting a just and peaceful world and of addressing non-democratic ideologies and movements are relevant not just to programmes dedicated to citizenship education, but are expected to pervade other curriculum areas including, explicitly, the teaching of languages. The Council of Europe recommends:

> encouraging multidisciplinary approaches and actions combining civic and political education with the teaching of history, philosophy, religions, languages, social sciences and all disciplines having a bearing on ethical, political, social, cultural or philosophical aspects, whether in terms of their actual content or the options or consequences involved for a democratic society. (Council of Europe, 2002: 3)

Although these policy guidelines have been developed at European meetings, they are in fact implementing commitments accepted in principle by all governments across the world. The Universal Declaration of Human Rights (UDHR) 1948 and the United Nations Convention on the Rights of the Child (CRC) 1989 form the basis of the agreed position of Member States of the United Nations. Both the Declaration and the Convention have articles detailing the purposes of education. The earlier formulation is as follows:

> Education shall be directed to the full development of the human personality and to the strengthening of respect for human rights and fundamental freedoms. It shall promote understanding, tolerance and friendship among all nations, racial or religious groups, and shall further the activities of the United Nations for the maintenance of peace. (Universal Declaration of Human Rights, Article 26.2)

The CRC is more detailed and includes the following aims for education:

■ The development of respect for human rights and fundamental freedoms, and for the principles enshrined in the Charter of the United Nations;

■ The development of respect for the child's parents, his or her own cultural identity, language and values, for the national values of the country in which the child is living, the country from which he or she may originate, and for civilisations different from his or her own;

■ The preparation of the child for responsible life in a free society, in the spirit of understanding, peace, tolerance, equality of sexes, and friendship among all peoples, ethnic, national and religious groups and persons of indigenous origin.

(United Nations Convention on the Rights of the Child, Article 29b, c, d)

There can be no doubt, given the voluntary but binding commitment of governments to the CRC, that there is, in principle, universal agreement about the importance of human rights education and of what can be encapsulated in the term intercultural education. Language education is clearly a significant opportunity to help learners develop 'respect for ...civilisations different from his or her own' and 'friendship among all peoples'.

Language education policies

It is increasingly recognised that language teaching and learning have aims that go beyond the merely instrumental. Language learning, even for business purposes, is part of a humanistic education that encourages intercultural communication on the basis of equality. At a European level, language education policy promotes the acquisition of plurilingual competence, seen as 'a condition and a constituent of democratic citizenship in Europe' (Beacco and Byram, 2003: 18). Language education policy is therefore developed in the context of EDC and this is explicitly spelt out in the Council of Europe's guide to language education policy.

> The teaching of languages has aims which are convergent with those of education for democratic citizenship: both are concerned with intercultural interaction and communication, the promotion of mutual understanding and the development of individual responsibility. (Beacco and Byram, 2003: 18)

This understanding of language education as a significant contributor to citizenship education is also acknowledged as underpinning language education policy in the UK at national levels. The national curriculum for England includes the following aims for the learning of languages:

> Through the study of foreign languages, pupils understand and appreciate different countries, cultures, people and communities – and as they do so, begin to *think of themselves as citizens of the world* as well as of the United Kingdom. (DfEE/QCA, 1999:14, my emphasis)

An alternative formulation to 'citizens of the world', offering a more comprehensive perspective that includes the local, the national and the global, is cosmopolitan citizenship (Osler and Vincent, 2002; Osler and Starkey, 2003 and 2005). In the same spirit, a high level report on the future of language teaching and learning in Britain recommended:

> Direct links should be established in school education between language learning and education for citizenship, so as to foster *notions of equality and acceptance of diversity* in children's minds at the earliest possible age. (Nuffield Languages Inquiry, 2000: 32, my emphasis)

This recommendation, whilst not mentioning human rights, refers specifically to the key human rights principles of equality and diversity. A Scottish report on languages, *Citizens of a Multilingual World*, also spells out this potential contribution to citizenship education:

> We consider that education in languages at school has an essential role to play in preparing all students for citizenship of the wider society. If it helps them become sensitive to the languages and cultures of others and develops in them sufficient confidence and competence to be able to use their languages, however modestly, in their interactions with other citizens, then we believe they are more likely to understand others and to be respected by them. In this way *the wider society becomes more open, democratic and inclusive.* (Ministerial Action Group on Languages, 2000: 2, my emphasis)

In spite of these emphatic statements of the role of language teaching in promoting democracy, the reality is that this is yet to be fully mainstreamed. Although there are many initiatives supporting this perspective, several of them described in this volume, the links between the language teaching agenda and the EDC agenda exist more at the level of rhetoric than reality. The British Council, whose influence in language teaching extends across the world, aspires to be both a world authority on English language teaching and to promote human rights and democracy (British Council, 2004). The Council has published useful studies on citizenship education and human rights education (Davies, 2000a and b; Chauhan, 2000). This marks the recognition by the British Council of the considerable possibilities for synergy between the hitherto separate agendas of English language teaching and EDC.

Challenges for language teachers

In order to mainstream and consolidate the role of language education within EDC, it is necessary to persuade teachers and learners of the practical advantages of adopting an intercultural rather than a purely instrumental approach. However, this may be difficult in situations where textbooks and course materials either fail to acknowledge a cultural dimension or present cultures in such a simplistic way as to stereotype them. In these circumstances teachers may need to provide their own materials or select them carefully from available published courses. Much recent course material still lacks adequate coverage of cultural content. Course writers frequently prioritise grammar and linguistic functions over social or political understanding.

A study of course materials available in Britain for teaching French as a foreign language reported that a number of courses are largely devoid of cultural references:

> Either in its format (for instance, its style of illustration, presentation of topics) or in its linguistic content (absence of specific societal markers within the language items), the material manages to retain a neutrality in cultural matters. In a few instances, it would be reasonable to say that some material focuses on a narrow view of British culture rather than encounters any French cultural aspects whatsoever. (Aplin, 2000: 8)

Such courses, which fail entirely to acknowledge that there is a cultural dimension to language teaching, also miss an opportunity to engage with and challenge language learners. They do nothing to combat stereotypes.

Even where courses include an explicit cultural dimension, basic stereotypes may remain and indeed be reinforced by the materials. Another study of learning materials found that:

> Reductionism is a problem inherent in all teaching material and it is all the more inevitable where the number of words available to cover a topic is sometimes limited to a few lines, particularly in specially written material. In such a context it is difficult to convey the diversity of cultural practices. (Fleig-Hamm, 1998, my translation)

Thus there are some textbooks that deny that studying a language necessarily means studying cultures and there are others that depict cultures so summarily that they fail to challenge learners. A culture presented as uniform and without complexity is likely to be stereotyped to the point of absurdity.

And yet research with language teachers suggests that many have a commitment to overcoming prejudice. They tend to see their role as conveying knowledge about a target culture (Byram and Risager, 1999). The purpose of studying other cultures is to encourage reflective learners. Where cultures are presented in their plurality and their complexity, students are helped to de-centre and relativise their relationship with their own culture of origin. In other words they reconsider their attitudes to what was previously considered foreign. This is one strategy for reducing xenophobia and overcoming prevalent stereotypes. Stereotyping involves labelling groups of people, usually in a negative way, according to preconceived ideas. It is often racist and is certainly undemocratic. It may be challenged in language learning, or reinforced.

It may be argued that the position of English is such that a cultural or intercultural dimension to English language teaching is less appropriate. Indeed the Council of Europe policy guidance identifies this challenge:

> The special position of English as a global lingua franca necessitates a different approach to the teaching of English. As a lingua franca it does not have as its main aim to enrich learners culturally but is above all considered as a skill whose perceived market value leads to social demand for it to be taught. (Beacco and Byram, 2003: 20)

In fact other evidence suggests that even in the case of English for business, where learners have a strongly instrumental view of language learning, an intercultural dimension may well be popular. The Chinese University of International Business and Economics provides language courses for its students and has concluded that:

> International business is an area that requires cultural sensitivity and responsiveness, and this is of paramount importance within joint ventures. Unfortunately, insensitivity and misplaced attitudes can cause business blunders. If we look at international business as a means to enhance mutual understanding and friendship, apart from profit-making, then the importance of cultural awareness cannot be over-estimated. (Zhenhua, 1999: 87)

Cultural awareness is an important element of language learning, certainly, but it needs to be critical cultural awareness. This has been defined as 'an ability to evaluate, critically and on the basis of explicit criteria, perspectives, practices and products in one's own and other cultures and countries' (Byram *et al.* 2002: 13). In making intercultural evaluative judgements, it is clearly appropriate to identify standards that, in principle, are able to command universal agreement. International human rights instruments provide such standards. Of particular importance to language teachers is the adoption of a position that acknowledges respect for human dignity and equality of human rights as the democratic basis for social interaction.

Without a frame of reference, comparisons between cultures, both within the learning group and between the learners and the target culture, may be the occasion for stereotypes, racist or sexist comments or jokes and derogatory remarks. These contradict the spirit of human rights, which is to be respectful of others. Stereotyping also negates the aims of education in general and of language learning in particular. A knowledge and understanding of human rights equips teachers and learners to engage with other cultures on the basis of equality of dignity.

Practical implications for language teachers

Adopting a human rights approach to language teaching provides a sound framework within which controversial issues can be examined. Debate is conducted showing respect for persons, particularly other interlocutors, as the essential dignity of human beings is acknowledged. Disparaging remarks about individuals or groups who are not present is also inappropriate behaviour and therefore unacceptable. On the other hand, if respect for human rights is regarded as a standard, judgements can be made about the words or actions of individuals, governments or cultural groups. In this way uncritical cultural relativism can be avoided. This perspective needs to be made explicit to the learners from the start and one way of addressing this is the study of human rights instruments in the target language. Such a study enables students to link the various topics they study to wider issues of human rights and is likely to prove interesting and popular (Starkey, 1996: 108).

The pedagogy associated with language learning provides many opportunities to develop citizenship skills as well as familiarise learners with key concepts associated with democracy. In many respects communicative methodology is in itself democratic. The skills developed in language classes are thus directly transferable to citizenship education.

> The communicative language classroom implies that priority is given to speech acts. The role of the teacher is to guide pupils in their use of the new communicative tool, the second language. Teachers will be concerned not just with linguistic achievements but with communicative competence as an end in itself. Skills (*savoir faire*) such as ability to listen, to reformulate the words of another the better to understand them, put a different point of view, produce a valid argument, conceding are all life skills (*savoir être*) with applicability elsewhere in school and in the outside world...The language class is a site where education for dialogue is especially developed. (Tardieu, 1999: 24, my translation)

In the communicative language classroom learners are often required to speak and discuss in pairs and groups, having the freedom to express their own opinions and develop ideas and new ways of thinking. This contribution to the overall project of democratic citizenship can also be recognised and developed. Since discussion and debate require working with others, taking part in public discourse and working to resolve conflicts, language teaching can contribute substantially to capacities for action and social competencies.

Whether the context is pair work, group work or discussions involving the whole class, teachers taking a human rights position insist on ground rules. This can help to ensure that expressions of opinion and conflicts of views are productive and not destructive. Guidance produced for teachers of citizenship in England gives the following advice that is also worth consideration for teachers of languages:

It is essential that pupils develop their own ground rules rather than be presented with ones produced elsewhere ... Pupils should be regularly reminded of the ground rules and their importance when handling sensitive issues appropriately during whole-class and group discussion.

The following ground rules are examples of ones established by pupils:

■ Listen to each other

■ Make sure everyone has a chance to speak

■ Don't use 'put downs' or make fun of what others say or do

■ Be helpful and constructive when challenging another's viewpoint

■ Offer help and support when it is needed

■ You have a right to 'pass' if you do not want to speak on an issue

■ Show appreciation when someone explains or does something well, or is helpful in some way to you.

(QCA, 2001: 38)

Although this guidance suggests that the ground rules should come from the pupils, and this is a possible activity for the language class in itself, teachers can of course feed in their own suggestions and might consider the following additional points:

■ Where a discussion is chaired, the authority of the chair is respected.

■ Even heated debates must be conducted in polite language.

■ Discriminatory remarks, particularly racist, sexist and homophobic discourse and expressions are totally unacceptable at any time.

■ Participants show respect when commenting on and describing people portrayed in visuals or texts.

■ All involved have the responsibility to challenge stereotypes.

■ A respectful tone is required at all times.

It goes without saying that, teachers are party to these agreements and will not use sarcasm, irony or disparaging judgements.

A move away from closed and true/false questions in reading and listening comprehension, to open-ended questions where opinions are genuinely sought and discussed can also invigorate language classes. When language teachers create a communication gap to provide for a more meaningful task, they should also try to encourage students to explore their differences of opinions as well as merely exchange information. Questioning by the language teacher and questions printed in textbooks may focus on language structures rather than on the truth. For example, one French course we examined asked students to manipulate a sentence to illustrate sequence of tenses following if. Starting from the given sentence: 'On the whole, if immigrant families speak French they adapt more easily to their new life', students were expected to produce the following sentences:

■ In years to come, if immigrant families speak French they will adapt more easily to their new life.

■ Historically, if immigrant families spoke French they adapted more easily to their new life.

■ Most people think that if immigrant families spoke French they would adapt more easily to their new life.

■ If immigrant families had spoken French on arrival, they would have adapted more easily to their new life.

(Starkey and Osler, 2001, our translation)

Although these sentences are correct grammatically, the exercise clearly reinforces the view that 'immigrant families' are inadequate and that in particular they are handicapped by lack of linguistic skills. In fact many families who come to settle in another country are bilingual. The exercise, suggesting a generalised language deficit, is thus misleading.

Although the course intended to present France in a positive light as a multicultural society, this example shows how the linguistic exploitation of the course material may counteract its socio-cultural objectives. The linguistic and cultural dimensions are meant to reinforce each other rather than one undermining the other. It would be quite possible to produce the same linguistic task whilst emphasising the capacities of the newcomers rather than their inadequacies. For instance the starting point could be: 'If French people are welcoming, immigrant families adapt more easily to their new life'.

Given the observance of ground rules and a climate of open debate with respect for other speakers, it is very much in the interests of the language teacher to promote controversy in the classroom. In debating issues that are meaningful to themselves and about which there are genuine differences of view, learners develop their linguistic fluency as they focus on the content of the debate rather than on the form of the language they are using.

Citizenship is about the public sphere and about understanding of and engagement with policies. It is not always the case, however, that language programmes of study encourage debate about real issues. A British report on the state of language teaching in schools noted that:

> the languages curriculum is perceived by students as *intrinsically* motivating to begin with through association with interesting and pleasurable activities at primary school but *that intrinsic motivation declines* at secondary school when students begin to perceive in it a lack of intellectual stimulation and a lack of deep engagement with their real and emerging adolescent interests. (Ministerial Action Group on Languages, 2000: 9, original emphasis).

These students have a negative attitude to language learning and one of the reasons for this may well be that the topics of study for languages are mainly associated with the private sphere. As such they fail to engage with political issues and lack intellectual stimulation for lively young minds. For instance, the topics prescribed for speaking examinations for sixteen-year-olds in England are:

- home life
- school life
- self, family and friends
- free time
- your local area
- careers, work, work experience
- holidays

(Oxford, Cambridge and RSA Examinations, 2000: 18)

The list of topics provides no encouragement to learners to look outside their own personal sphere. Even interest in the target culture can only be evoked in the context of holidays. For one teacher, this limited conception of language learning directly contributes to lack of engagement by the learners.

> Perhaps the biggest problem (and the main cause of boredom) is that those topics are visited and revisited year after year adding on a little more vocabulary each time. (Callaghan, 1998: 6)

One consequence is that the learning of languages may lack broad appeal. It can be argued that the majority of topics in the above examination syllabus appeal to girls rather than boys, though several are equally disliked by both sexes. For example one teacher found that 'home life' was enjoyed by girls, who liked to describe room furnishings in detail. The boys tended merely to list items of electrical equipment. Family and home life tends to include descriptions of household tasks. However, the teacher noted that girls are much more likely to have experience of these tasks than boys. She concludes:

> Children are taught to speak a language as if they lived in a moral vacuum and that the only interactions they are likely to have are with shopkeepers ... This sanitised version of life makes French particularly unpalatable to boys who, on the whole, prefer realism and facts. (Callaghan,1998: 6)

She suggests that if the teaching was re-structured to include a debate on the gendering of household tasks, this could include both groups more equally and promote some awareness of equality issues.

Many courses use scenarios that invite learners to imagine visiting a country associated with the target language and attempt to give the learner a role as actor in an intercultural setting. However, since the purpose imagined for the visit is often tourism, the language learner is often represented in course material not as citizen but as child within the family, pupil within the school and consumer within society. There is rarely a suggestion that students will take with them any curiosity or any social, historical, economic or political awareness.

A logical response to negativity and low motivation may well be consciously to introduce the public sphere and give a citizenship dimension to the topics. Even themes that appear very personal and even trivial can be given a political dimension. For instance, within 'leisure time' the theme of sport can be examined from a number of perspectives including:

> Gender – are there sports that are predominantly played by men or by women? Is this changing? What are the pressures for change?

> Age – are there sports for younger people and for older people? What can be done to help young people or older people practise sport in order to improve or maintain their health?

> Region – are there local sports? Do learners identify with local teams? Do some teams have specific cultural traditions or origins (e.g. founded by a trade union or a religious organisation)?

> Religion – are there religious objections to playing sport, or days when some people choose not to do sport because of religious observance?

> Racism – is this found in spectator sports? Are the players of foreign teams or foreign players in local teams always treated with respect? Is there an organised campaign against racism in sport?

Other common themes such as food, homes, school, tourism and leisure can be treated with a similarly critical perspective (Starkey, 2002a and b; Starkey and Osler 2003).

Conclusion

Given the importance of motivation to language learning, the engagement of learners is crucial and this may well be best achieved by providing opportunities to learn citizenship knowledge and skills whilst learning the language. The Council of Europe Recommendation on EDC suggests learning outcomes, all of which can be promoted through language learning. These include learners developing the ability to:

■ settle conflicts in a non-violent manner

■ argue in defence of one's viewpoint

■ listen to, understand and interpret other people's arguments

■ recognise and accept differences

■ make choices, consider alternatives and subject them to ethical analysis

■ shoulder shared responsibilities

■ establish constructive, non-aggressive relations with others

■ develop a critical approach to information, thought patterns and philosophical, religious, social, political and cultural concepts, at the same time remaining committed to fundamental values and principles of the Council of Europe.

(Council of Europe, 2002:3)

However, the Recommendation also stresses that these learning outcomes are most likely to be achieved through diversified educational methods and approaches in a democratic environment. This has profound implications for the organisation of language learning and of educational institutions. For instance, it entails:

■ active participation of pupils, students, educational staff and parents in democratic management of the learning place, in particular, the educational institution

■ the promotion of the democratic ethos in educational methods and relationships formed in a learning context

■ learner-centred methods, including project pedagogics based on adopting a joint, shared objective and fulfilling it in a collective manner, whether such projects are defined by a class, a school, the local, regional, national, European or international community, or by the various civil society organisations involved in education for democratic citizenship (non-governmental organisations, enterprises, professional organisations)

■ encouraging exchanges, meetings and partnerships between pupils, students and teachers from different schools so as to improve mutual understanding between individuals.

(Council of Europe, 2002:4)

The training and professional development of language teachers has tended to concentrate on how to teach languages rather than what to teach. The methodology of language teaching is potentially democratic as it involves maximising communication between learners rather than communication being controlled by the teacher. However, language teachers also have to consider what their role is in helping learners acquire knowledge as well as skills. As the case studies in this volume illustrate, there are many opportunities to promote education for democratic citizenship through language teaching. In fact, the learning of languages takes on real meaning and significance when it is seen as part of learning for democracy. Language learning to promote intercultural competence is a key component of education for democratic citizenship.

References

Aplin, R. (2000) Images of France: cultural awareness in French language teaching materials, *Francophonie* 22: 6-10.

Beacco, J-C. and Byram, M. (2003) *Guide for the Development of Language Education Policies in Europe: from linguistic diversity to plurilingual education. Executive Version.* Strasbourg: Council of Europe Language Policy Division.

British Council (2004) *Strategy 2010: our vision for the future.* London: British Council.

Byram, M., Gribkova, B. and Starkey, H. (2002) *Developing the Intercultural Dimension in Language Teaching: a practical introduction for teachers.* Strasbourg: Council of Europe, Language Policy Division.

Byram, M. and Risager, K. (1999) *Language Teachers, Politics and Cultures.* Clevedon: Multilingual Matters.

Callaghan, M. (1998) An investigation into the causes of boys' underachievement in French, *Language Learning Journal,* 17: 2-7.

Chauhan, L. (2000) *Citizenship Education and Human Rights Education: developments and resources in the UK.* London: British Council.

Council of Europe (2002) *Recommendation (2002) 12 of the Committee of Ministers to Member States on Education for Democratic Citizenship* (Adopted by the Committee of

Ministers on 16 October 2002 at the 812th meeting of the Ministers' Deputies) Strasbourg: Council of Europe. http://www.coe.int/T/e/Cultural_Cooperation/Education/E.D.C/ Documents_and_publications/By_Type/Adopted_texts/092_recommendation_2002_12.asp# TopOfPage accessed 5 October 2004

Davies, L. (2000a) *Citizenship Education and Human Rights Education: key concepts and debates.* London: British Council.

Davies, L. (2000b) *Citizenship Education and Human Rights Education: an international overview.* London: British Council.

Department for Education and Employment/Qualifications and Curriculum Authority (1999) *The National Curriculum for England.* London: DfEE.

Fleig-Hamm, C. (1998) La francophonie dans les manuels de français langue seconde: apports et limites, *La revue canadienne des langues vivantes,* 54 (4). http://www.utpjournals. com/jour.ihtml?lp=product/cmlr/544/544-Fleig.html

Ministerial Action Group on Languages (2000) *Citizens of a Multilingual World.* Edinburgh: Scottish Executive Education Department.

Nuffield Languages Inquiry (2000) *Languages: the next generation.* London: Nuffield Foundation.

Osler, A. (2005) Education for democratic citizenship: new challenges in a globalised world, in: A. Osler and H. Starkey (eds.) *Citizenship and Language Learning: international perspectives.* Stoke-on-Trent: Trentham.

Osler, A. and Starkey, H. (2003) Learning for cosmopolitan citizenship: theoretical debates and young people's experiences, *Educational Review,* 55(3): 243-254.

Osler, A. and Starkey, H. (2005) *Changing Citizenship: democracy and inclusion in education.* Buckingham: Open University Press.

Osler, A. and Vincent, K. (2002) *Citizenship and the Challenge of Global Education.* Stoke-on-Trent: Trentham.

Oxford, Cambridge and RSA Examinations (2000) *OCR GCSEs in French, German, Spanish and Gujerati.* http://www.ocr.org.uk/

Qualifications and Curriculum Authority (QCA) (2001) *Citizenship: a scheme of work for key stage 3. Teacher's guide.* London: QCA.

Starkey, H (1996) Intercultural education through foreign language learning: a human rights approach in: A. Osler, H-F. Rathenow and H. Starkey (eds.) *Teaching for Citizenship in Europe.* Stoke-on-Trent: Trentham.

Starkey, H. (2002a) *Democratic Citizenship, Languages, Diversity and Human Rights.* Strasbourg: Council of Europe Language Policy Division.

Starkey, H. (2002b) Language teaching, citizenship, human rights and intercultural education, in: A. Swarbrick (Ed.), *Modern Foreign Languages in Secondary Schools.* London: RoutledgeFalmer.

Starkey, H. and Osler, A. (2001) Language learning and antiracism: some pedagogical challenges, *Curriculum Journal,* 12 (3): 313-329.

Starkey, H., and Osler, A. (2003) Language teaching for cosmopolitan citizenship, in: K. Brown and M. Brown (eds.) *Reflections on Citizenship in a Multilingual World.* London: Centre for Information on Language Teaching.

Tardieu, C. (1999) *Le Professeur Citoyen.* Bourg-la-Reine: Editions M.T.

Torney-Purta, J., Schwille, J. and Amadeo, J. (1999) *Civic Education across Countries.* Amsterdam: International Association for the Evaluation of Educational Achievement.

Zhenhua, H. (1999) The impact of globalisation on English in Chinese universities, in: D. Graddol and U. Meinhof (eds) *English in a Changing World.* Milton Keynes: Catchline/ AILA.

3

Representing Britain as a diverse society:
the work of the British Council

Robin Richardson

In 1943 the poet John Betjeman was asked to give a talk on the BBC Home Service entitled 'why we are fighting'. He said that the war was in defence of England and that for him:

> England stands for the Church of England, eccentric incumbents, oil-lit churches, Women's Institutes, modest village inns, arguments about cow-parsley on the altar, the noise of mowing machines on Saturday afternoons, local newspapers, local auctions, the poetry of Tennyson, Crabbe, Hardy and Matthew Arnold, local talent, local concerts, a visit to the cinema, branch-line trains, light railways, leaning on gates and looking across fields ... I know the England I want to come home to is not very different from that in which you want to live. If it were some efficient ant-heap which the glass and steel, flat-roof, straight-roof boys want to make it, then how could we love it as we do? (quoted in Richardson and Miles, 2003: 60)

Several decades later, many of Betjeman's icons are clearly outdated. The underlying vision of a good society, however, remains attractive – a society marked by gentleness, courtesy, civility, respect for privacy, tolerance of eccentricity, attention to all that is modest, local and human-scale. It contains also a fine emphasis on the local – 'local newspapers, local auctions, local talent, local concerts, branch-line trains...'.

Betjeman also valuably stressed the importance of symbols, for it is through symbols, icons and imagery that the citizens crystallise a sense of who they are and where they belong. The essential problem with his picture was that he selected symbols which omitted and indeed excluded large numbers of people and experiences. Particularly obviously, he omitted all citizens who were not English. It was the British, not the English, Broadcasting Corporation for which he was working; and the British, not the English, armed services that were fighting in the war. Nevertheless all his icons were English. Further, he omitted everyone who was not associated with the Church of England and anyone who lived in a city or conurbation. Even more seriously and outrageously, though in time of war not surprisingly, he omitted knowledge and experiences of internal conflict and change. To imply that squabbles about cow parsley on the altar are epitomes of disagreement in British society is perverse, to put it mildly. One only has to recall, for example, Ian McEwan's novel *Atonement*, set in the very period out of which Betjeman was speaking, to be reminded that the green and pleasant land of Britain was torn then as always by ravages of class and gender, and that all narratives about nation and nationality are deeply problematic (Runnymede Trust, 2000).

It is interesting to compare Betjeman's portrait with a much more recent attempt to represent Britain. In Tel Aviv in autumn 2001 there was a showcase exhibition of contemporary British culture at the Herzliya Museum of Modern Art. The title was *No World Without You: reflections of identity in new British art.* In an article in the catalogue, the curator explained that all the works on display had in common 'the search for our Significant Other, without whom we cannot form our own self-identity', for 'a self does not exist, save through interactions with others'. The exhibition recognised, and indeed put centre-stage, the experiences of women and issues of gender identity. It recognised too the struggles of creative artists to find and claim their identity through the intricacies and endless ambiguities of self-expression. A flavour of the imagery is provided by extracts from the exhibition catalogue. One can see at a glance that the icons representing Britain were remarkably different from those which had been chosen by Betjeman:

> Sarah Jones explores relationships in British society and within the family through figures of adolescent girls in their shiny polished rooms in their middle class homes. The frozen lifeless expressions of these beautiful girls are tantamount to an extension and enhancement of the setting in which they live ... In these rooms adolescent dreams are woven ... Nevertheless, there is a distinct feeling that these girls will eventually, quite predictably, choose the comfortable bourgeois option, just like their mothers did.

Hannah Starkey's photographs ... [originate] in the perception that women, to a much greater extent than men, tend to observe, watch, diagnose. Viewing and analysis are identified as female properties, observing others as a way to learn about ourselves. The photographs depict women looking in the mirror, women observing each other, or women whose attention is drawn to someone outside the picture plane.

Sam Taylor-Wood's ... works in the exhibition are taken from the series Third Party. It is not coincidental that the party was chosen as a back-drop for her pieces. A party is a place where seduction and alienation, jealousy and oblivion, light and darkness, the unexpected and the predictable all blend together. As a scene of action it reinforces and illuminates the problematic nature of human relationships.

Sophy Rickett employs night-time as the setting and essence of her works ... the night and the bridge are intermediate states, places that conceal different entities, both male and female, sites where gender identity becomes blurred.

Elisa Sighicelli's photographs are created in domestic settings that are introverted, intimate and uninhabited. They convey a sense of sadness. A feeling of monotonous routine, loneliness and alienation emanates from the semi-lit rooms. (Gottlib, 2001)

The curator remarked on a further aspect of diverse and changing Britain: 'world attention and the receptiveness of international audiences have been fuelled, *inter alia*, by the incredible cultural diversity of British youth. In the light of this observation, it is relevant and sobering to note that of the thirteen artists featured in the exhibition, eleven were women, twelve live and work in London and all thirteen were white. The 'incredible cultural diversity of British youth' was, simply, invisible: not recognised as relevant to the con-struction of self-identity or to interactions between self and other. In this respect at least, Betjeman would have felt at home.

The representation of Britain in Tel Aviv raised two sets of questions. First, and more obviously: through which symbols, icons, archetypes and micro-cosms should Britain be represented, both to itself and to others? Second: who should decide this, and how? The second of these questions is about the decision-making and selection processes within the structures and contacts of the British Council (BC) which led to this particular outcome; and about the ways they need to be modified to ensure that a similar outcome is un-likely to occur again. The problem is not that there are insufficient talented Asian and black artists, but that too many gatekeepers and senior arts administrators, being white, do not promote them. The issue here is not to do with statistical accuracy, but with redressing historical imbalances and countering marginalisation and invisibility.

The episode was a striking example of what the Stephen Lawrence Inquiry report (Macpherson, 1999), using a term coined in the United States in the 1960s, called institutional racism. The Inquiry team provided their own description of this and also quoted many others. One of the clearest and fullest accounts from others was from oral evidence by members of the Black Police Association:

> The term institutional racism should be understood to refer to the way an institution or organisation may systematically or repeatedly treat, or tend to treat, people differently because of their race. So ... we are not talking about individuals in the service, who may be unconscious as to the nature of what they are doing, but about the net effect of what they do.

> A second source of institutional racism is our culture ... How and why does that impact on black individuals on the street? Well, we would say the occupational culture within the police service, given the fact that the majority of police officers are white, tends to be the white experience, the white beliefs, the white values.

> Given that these predominantly white officers only meet members of the black community in confrontational situations, they tend to stereotype black people in general. This can lead to all sorts of negative views and assumptions about black people, so we should not underestimate the occupational culture within the police service as being a primary source of institutional racism in the way we differentially treat black people.

> Interestingly I say we because there is no marked difference between black and white in the force essentially. We are all consumed by this occupational culture. Some of us may think we rise above it on some occasions, but generally speaking we tend to conform to the norms of the occupational culture, [for it's] ... all powerful in shaping our views and perceptions of a particular community. (Macpherson, 1999: 6.28)

To address institutional racism, the black police officers were in effect saying, you have to look at two separate things and at the interaction between them: on the one hand, the net effects of an organisation on the outside world; on the other, the occupational culture of an organisation in its internal workings. The net effect of the BC decision in the Tel Aviv exhibition was twofold. Visitors to the exhibition were misled and misinformed about modern British society. An opportunity was missed to foster the careers and profile of Black-British and Asian-British artists.

Representing Britain

The BC is aware that it needs to study and modify the ways in which it represents Britain as a diverse society. In 2002 it commissioned an evaluation of its programmes and operations in this respect. This chapter continues by describing how the evaluation was conducted and concludes by summarising its recommendations (Richardson, 2002).

The BC's overall aims are 'to win recognition for the United Kingdom's values, ideas and achievements; and 'to nurture lasting, mutually beneficial relationships with other countries'. To what extent and in what ways, as it pursues these two broad aims, does the British Council adequately represent the diversity of the UK? This was the fundamental question considered by the evaluation. It was studied with regard to five separate ways in which the UK is diverse: race and ethnicity; gender; disability; the UK's four nations; England's nine regions. The first three of these were chosen because there is legislation about them in Britain. The fourth was chosen because, partly in the light of recent administrative, legislative and governmental changes in Britain as a result of devolution, the BC has a formal commitment to representing all four of the UK's nations and, when appropriate, all of England's regions. In relation to each of these five aspects of diversity, the same set of generic questions may be asked:

- What are the UK values, ideas and achievements for which the BC seeks recognition, and on the basis of which it seeks to nurture lasting relationships with other countries?

- What does the BC do well in this regard, and what are the principles underlying its successes?

- What problems, difficulties and tensions does it encounter?

- What could it and should it do better?

These generic questions were asked with regard to BC operations in two countries in particular, Israel and South Africa. Visits were made to the BC offices in Tel Aviv and West Jerusalem, and in Cape Town, Johannesburg and Pretoria. Interviews and meetings were held with both staff and partners, and a wide range of documentation was collected and studied. In Israel it was in addition possible to administer a brief questionnaire about images and impressions of Britain.

In pursuing its twofold purpose of (a) winning recognition abroad for the UK's values, ideas and achievements, and (b) nurturing lasting, mutually beneficial relationships with other countries, the Council has proposed distinctions between four levels of knowledge and involvement. The four levels are summarised by the terms (1) influence (2) engagement (3) appreciation and (4) awareness. Figure 3.1 opposite shows how the generic questions were asked in relation to issues of race and ethnicity.

'What the Council should do,' said someone in an interview during this evaluation, 'is conduct a robust debate about the nature of multiculturalism. It's not enough to repeat the mantra 'Britain is a multicultural society'. For what does that mean exactly? We cannot represent Britain as a multicultural society if we're not clear what a multicultural society actually is, and whether it's a good thing or an unfortunate thing'. In another interview someone referred to the word diversity: 'Why is the Council using the word diversity? Is it because it's a nicer, gentler term than equality? Is the Council afraid of talking about hard issues such as racism, prejudice and cultural bias?'

This chapter is not an appropriate place for a lengthy discussion of essential core concepts, or for a substantial contribution to the robust debate that the one person quoted above requested. A brief comment, however, will be relevant, and will help clarify the approaches and assumptions on which the evaluation as a whole was based. The first thing to say is that, yes, the term diversity seems to many people softer, more comfortable, less threatening, than terms such as equality and racism. The assumed dichotomy here between equality and diversity, however, is false. Both concepts are essential and neither is complete without the other. For it is as unjust to treat people similarly when in relevant respects they are different as it is to treat them differently when in relevant respects they are similar. This is particularly obvious in matters relating to gender and disability – it can be unjust to treat women as if in all respects their life-experiences, needs and interests are the same as those of men, and vice versa, and it can be unjust not to make reasonable adjustments and accommodations to take account of the needs of people with disabilities.

In the fields of inter-ethnic, inter-cultural and inter-racial relationships, it can similarly be unjust to be 'colour-blind' or 'difference-blind', for not all people have the same narratives, life-experiences, perceptions and frames of reference. The UK government has recently adopted the semantic device of using both terms – diversity and equality – in official discourse (Office of the Deputy Prime Minister, 2001). This usage was pioneered in local government

Level	Nature	**Principal** and subsidiary questions
4	AWARENESS	**Are MOST users, contacts and partners made aware that the UK is diverse in terms of race and cultural diversity?**
		Is ethnic diversity represented in the visual environment at Council offices, particularly in reception areas; in the contents and design of the Council's newsletters and publicity material; in material about Britain provided as free handouts; in the images and references in ELT materials; and on country websites?
		Are Asian British and Black British consultants, performers, teachers and lecturers represented amongst visitors taken overseas by the Council?
		When the Council brings people to the UK, are there Asian British and Black British people amongst those whom they meet?
3	APPRECIATION	**Are MANY users, contacts and partners helped to appreciate that there is significant expertise in the UK in relation to issues of race equality and cultural diversity?**
		Do they have opportunities to see Asian British and Black British performers and artists?
		Is appreciation fostered not only of actions by government but also of the concerns and campaigns of NGOs, and of current and recent research and reflection in academia?
		Is appreciation fostered in free informational handouts provided by the Council; in ELT materials; in proactive information services?
		When people are brought to the UK by the Council, do they visit institutions and organisations where there is significant experience and expertise on race and diversity issues?
2	ENGAGEMENT	**Do SEVERAL users, contacts and partners interact and communicate personally with specialists in or from the UK in relation to race and diversity issues?**
		Is learning in these interactions mutual, not one-way?
1	INFLUENCE	**Do CERTAIN users, contacts and partners use their knowledge and experience of diversity in the UK to influence and modify policy-making and decision-making in their own country?**
		For example, as senior politicians and civil servants; as journalists and other influence-leaders; as senior managers in the public, private and NGO sectors; and as arts administrators?
		Do certain visual and performing artists incorporate insights and techniques from cultural diversity in the UK into new work?

Figure 3.1: Ethnicity: issues for evaluation and review of the work of the British Council

and in the private sector. Pragmatic reasons for adopting it are provided by the EU Employment Directive, which became mandatory throughout the EU from December 2003.

The Canadian political philosopher Charles Taylor has argued that in all considerations of equality and diversity a key concept is that of recognition. He writes:

> Identity is partly shaped by recognition or its absence, often by the misrecognition of others, and so a person or group of people or society can suffer real damage, real distortion, if the people or society around them mirror back to them a confining or demeaning or contemptible picture of themselves. Nonrecognition or misrecognition can inflict harm, can be a form of oppression, imprisoning someone in a false, distorted and reduced mode of being. (Taylor, 1992: 25)

A further essential concept in this context, implied by Taylor's reference to recognition, is that of social cohesion. Just as neither equality nor diversity is a sufficient moral value in itself, so also do both need to be complemented and qualified by notions of cohesion and belonging. A democracy such as Britain needs not only to uphold the values of equality and diversity, but also to be held together by certain shared values and – so far as is feasible – by certain shared imagery, symbols and stories.

This is not the same as claiming, as Betjeman appeared to do in his 1943 broadcast, that Britishness is of long standing, or that British stories and symbols are static and non-negotiable. The reality is that the balance between equality, diversity and cohesion has always been a contest and that settlements have always been provisional. Britain has always contained competing perceptions, narratives and interests. There have been disagreements and negotiations related to class, gender, language, religion, region and nation. The emphasis that British identity and self-understanding are continually being negotiated and re-defined has notably been made by the British Studies movement, pioneered and significantly supported by the BC in many countries throughout the world. It can only become more important in years to come, with the mutually reinforcing pressures of globalisation, European integration, devolution from Westminster and Whitehall, migration, and increased social and moral pluralism. This is the context in which the BC seeks to win recognition for the 'values, ideas and achievements', to quote again its mission statement, of the UK.

A recent piece of attitudinal research set the background for the evaluation. It was carried out by Mori in 1999 and 2000 and took place with the successor generation (young professionals aged 24-35 likely to rise to positions of influence in their society) in 28 different countries (Ratcliffe with Griffin, 1999; Ratcliffe, 2000). In relation to the representation of diversity within the UK, the principal findings and reflections included those which are shown in the quotations below:

> Young people have an ambivalent view of Britain. On the whole they see it as fair, caring and democratic, but also as divided by class and, in the eyes of some, racially intolerant. Promoting an image of the UK as a multicultural society will demonstrate a new and more attractive face of the UK to the world, and this may also help dispel other negative and outdated images.'

> The general image of the UK around the world is that it is reliable but dull, and this image is often quite deeply rooted. To contradict it, we need to identify what young people already know or what they already want, and work with that. Shocking them into something they 'ought' to know or want will not work. Then we need to state the message and restate it consistently, and make sure that every other message that we are giving out supports it.

> Young people are critical of Britain's social relationships and do not re-gard us as especially creative or innovative. In general, they respect us more than they like us, and they find America more attractive. We are seen as cold, condescending and unwelcoming towards visitors and foreigners. Respondents in Commonwealth countries attribute our coldness to an atavistic colonial mindset, and in other countries we are similarly seen as hanging on to notions of past superiority.

> The UK's reputation in the arts is seen to lie more in past than present achievements.(Ratcliffe, 2000: 7, 9, 11, 43)

The UK is seen as having strong traditions and a well-developed sense of heritage and identity. But the report concludes that tradition is not only a major asset but also the principal liability. The overall conclusion drawn from the Mori research was that: 'Reinforcing the positives and combating the negatives in these perceptions will require considerable and sustained effort' (Ratcliffe, 2000: 9). The findings are sobering, for they show clearly that attempts to win recognition for UK values, ideas and achievements in re-lation to equality and diversity are likely to be met with considerable scep-ticism.

In this evaluation, negative perceptions of Britain such as those outlined above were frequently made in the interviews and discussions, particularly in South Africa. A questionnaire was administered that took the form of a 'semantic differential' test. It presented several pairs of statements about Britain, with one item in the pair being negative and the other positive. Respondents were asked to show their own view on the spectrum by using a seven-point scale. Some of the items were to do with diversity; some were to do with tradition and innovation. There were seven pairs of items to do with diversity, as follows:

Sexist, patriarchal	Equality between the sexes
Much racial discrimination	Fair treatment of minorities
Stiff, reserved, distant people	Warm, friendly, open people
Christian, all-white	Multi-faith, multicultural
Disabled people are neglected	Good provision for disabled
Dominated by London	Much regional variety
Hostile to foreigners	Welcoming to foreigners

There were eight pairs of items about tradition and innovation, shown below.

Obsessed with past history	Progressive and changing
Little innovation in the arts	Exciting creativity in the arts
Old-fashioned, traditional	Forward-looking, young
Ruled by an elite class	Equality and democracy
No progress recently in science	Good recent science
Little individual freedom	Sound respect for human rights
Getting worse	Getting better
Stale and out-of-date	Source of fresh ideas

On both of these dimensions three groups in Israel were basically positive: a class of English language students, the whole staff group at the Jerusalem office, and a group of women's officers in the civil service. Much less positive attitudes were expressed by a group of Palestinian Arabs in Israel, and by a group of black people in South Africa.

It would be valuable if Mori or a similar organisation were to be commissioned to investigate, using scientifically random samples and appropriate factor analysis, the extent to which the two dimensions are (a) internally coherent and (b) genuinely independent of each other. In the absence of empirical evidence on these matters, it seems reasonable to speculate that two separate dimensions do exist, even if the actual items cited above do not adequately capture them. If they are pictured as separate continuums, a 2 x 2 matrix can be pictured, depicting four general orientations towards Britain. The matrix is shown in Figure 3.2.

The Council's aim, in the terms of the admittedly schematic and abstract terms of Figure 3.2, is to shift perceptions from orientation 1, Britain seen as

	1. Britain seen as traditional	2. Britain seen as creative
Britain seen as uniform	1	3
Britain seen as diverse	2	4

Figure 3.2: Four possible orientations towards Britain

both uniform and traditional, to orientation 4, Britain seen as both diverse and innovative. Figure 3.2 suggests that there are two possible routes, so to speak, from orientation 1 to orientation 4 – either via 2 or else via 3, rather than all in one go. This notion of routes is particularly relevant in view of Mori's stern warning that currently there are strong negative views of Britain amongst influential young people. If at least they can be moved from 1 to 2 or from 1 to 3, they are more likely, it is reasonable to speculate, to end up eventually at 4.

The difference between orientations 2 and 3 can be illustrated with regard to a recent project supported by the BC in Israel. The project involved a touring production of *Titus Andronicus*. One of the actors was black, and therefore a traditional representation of Britain – a Shakespeare play – was combined with modern multiculturalism. To this extent the production was an example of orientation 2. The black actor played the part of a villain in the play, and this implied that Britain is sufficiently mature as a multicultural society to face the racist stereotypes of black people that have disfigured British culture over the centuries. In this respect too, the production was an example of 2. But in other respects, the production was an example of 3. For the production was highly creative theatrically, and its themes of revenge and spiralling violence were poignantly and brilliantly evocative of issues in contemporary Israeli society and politics. The inclusion of a black actor in the cast, and the powerful confrontation with racism in British culture that his portrayal of a villain subliminally but inescapably triggered, meant that the overall message of the performance was what Figure 3.2 calls orientation 4 – Britain was vividly portrayed as *both* creative *and* diverse. In the four key terms of Figure 3.1, it promoted awareness, appreciation and engagement and almost certainly promoted influence as well.

The evaluation came across many other examples of excellent practice in the Council's work, both actually and potentially. These included film programmes, dance projects, participation in conferences, study visits and educational exchanges. The diversity in these examples tended to be about issues of gender and disability, however, rather than about race and ethnicity. Also, as in the case of the art exhibition in Tel Aviv, the evaluation found examples of opportunities being missed. The flavour of these is given below, in an account of visual materials.

One of the ways the Council represents Britain is through publications of the Foreign and Commonwealth Office. They display these on the walls of their offices; make them available in their offices as free handouts; and sometimes include them in delegates' packs at conferences and events. The materials are attractively and expensively produced and are used also in English language teaching (ELT), either directly or else as background context. They give messages to BC staff themselves, of course, as well as to customers and contacts outside. The following notes give an idea of issues which the materials raise within the context of considering BC representation of Britain as a diverse society.

> ### The United Kingdom: Ten Centuries in the Making
> In the small print at the foot of this large wall-chart, it is indicated that it was published in April 1994. It is only since 1994, by and large, that scholarly work and controversies to do with the making of Britain and construction of Britishness over the centuries has become widely known outside academia. So it is not surprising that the poster does not reflect such work. There is a clear statement verbally that the United Kingdom did not come into existence until 1801 and that in its current form it dates only since 1922. But the unmistakable message visually, communicated through the colouring, imagery, design and composition, is of a thousand years of unbroken history, symbolised by a single royal family down the centuries.
>
> The poster marks clearly the civil war of the mid-seventeenth century but otherwise implies that the only political changes during the last thousand years have been the transitions from Norman to Plantagenet and then from Plantagenet to Tudor and so on to the Windsors. There is not a single visual reference to Ireland, Scotland or Wales, and the only verbal references to these other countries on the main part of the chart are to Ireland in the sixteenth century and to Wales in the thirteenth. The high-profile references to the British Empire have a hollow ring when considered alongside, for example, the Mori research on views of Britain in other countries (see above), or the sceptical views of Britain amongst black South Africans and Palestinian Arabs that were encountered in interviews and discussions.

Festivals in Britain

This wall-chart, the same size as the one mentioned above, was published in March 1999. It gives great prominence to the Notting Hill Carnival and to Diwali, and there are pictures also (though smaller) of the Halloween Carnival at Derry City, Londonderry; the Braemar Highland Games Gathering in Scotland; the Royal National Eistedfodd; the Appleby Horse Fair (attracting 'thousands of Romanies and travelling people') and Eid-ud-Fitr. The two large images which balance Notting Hill and Diwali, however, are of something called the Straw Bear ceremony that takes place one day in January each year in a small village in Cambridgeshire and of 1930s holidays at the seaside. The chart is certainly multicultural, but arguably implies through its juxtapositions that all the customs it depicts are merely quaint and old-fashioned, and irrelevant to real life. The depiction of cultural and national diversity in the imagery gives little or no sense of a country that is modern, progressive and innovative. And certainly there is no sense of institutional racism (see above) In the ways that images of Britain are selected.

England

This booklet was published in summer 2000. It has 24 pages, and is remarkably well designed and presented. There is reference to 'the diverse backgrounds and traditions of ethnic peoples [sic] who have made their home in Britain', but the imagery implies that the distinctive thing about so-called ethnic peoples is that they have dark skins and colourful clothes and customs. There is a small photograph of Linford Christie breaking the tape in the 100 metres final at the world athletics championships, but there are more black people in this small picture (all the other finalists were black as well) than in all the other illustrations in the booklet put together. There are far more images of trees, fields and country villages than of cities, and the last large image in the booklet is of a cricket bat. It is unfortunate that the fine design and high-quality illustrations should be accompanied by conceptually impoverished text ('ethnic peoples'), and that a wider range of cultural and intellectual expertise was not drawn on in the original planning.

Recommendations

The recommendations from the evaluation were summarised as follows:

Management planning and review

In all planning there should be attention to diversity issues. In this respect, the questions set out Figure 3.1 can be adapted for use in a range of BC offices throughout the world, to alert senior managers to key issues before plans become difficult or impossible to change. Senior managers also need to consider how information services can systematically contribute a diversity dimension to all aspects of the Council's work. At its headquarters offices in Britain, the Council should set up a proactive information service on equality and diversity issues.

Debate and deliberation

The concepts of diversity, equality and representation need to be fully discussed in BC publications and training events. For example, the Council should support and promote fuller debate on the nature of multiculturalism, both in Britain and in other countries, and about the issues of personal, cultural and national identity that arise. Often such debate should be informed by the concerns and themes of British Studies. Amongst many other topics, there needs to be further academic and cross-cultural debate about the nature and importance of contemporary dance; and about developments in educational policy, particularly around multicultural and anti-racist education, and citizenship and human rights education.

Arts and creativity

It is particularly important to mainstream diversity values and themes into projects, which showcase British creativity in the arts. It is in any case essential that the BC play an influential role in challenging institutional bias in arts administration in the UK.

Training and professional development

Information services need training for new roles connected with research and with being proactive, and this is particularly important with regard to diversity and equality issues. There are also clear professional development needs if ELT is to take on a measure of explicit responsibility for influencing understandings and perceptions of diversity in the UK. BC training events, particularly those that are arranged for senior managers, should include skills in addressing and managing racialised conflicts in the workplace. Much or most staff training on diversity issues should contain debate and deliberation, as mentioned above, but also should be closely connected to planning, programming and evaluating actual BC work.

UK participation in events

When the BC organises major seminars overseas on issues relating to diversity and equality, participation by UK delegates should be by application rather than, or as well as, invitation. Targets should be set for the UK representation: for example, at least one half women, equal numbers of Asian, black and white people, and at least a quarter from Northern Ireland, Scotland and Wales. It should be recognised in this regard that representation of diversity is not to do with statistical accuracy but with redressing historical imbalances, marginalisation and invisibility.

Visits to the UK
When the Council organises study visits to the UK it is important that participants should meet with NGOs as well as with officialdom. Partnerships with UK institutions should include reference to diversity and equality issues in statements about expectations and requirements.

Looking forward
Insofar as the Council is able to implement these recommendations it will increasingly distance itself from the chocolate-box and self-deceiving notions of Britain evoked in John Betjeman's radio broadcast in 1943. The processes of implementation will necessarily involve discomfort and probably even pain. The strengths and successes of the Council are such that the discomfort and pain will not be intolerable. A truer picture of Britain will be given not only to the outside world but also to the British themselves.

References
Gottlib, N. (2001) *No World Without You: reflections of identity in new British art.* (Exhibition catalogue). Tel Aviv: Herzliya Museum of Modern Art.

Macpherson, W. (1999) *The Stephen Lawrence Inquiry.* London: The Stationery Office.

Office of the Deputy Prime Minister (2001) *Towards Equality and Diversity: implementing the employment and race directives. Consultation document.* http://www.dti.gov.uk/er/equality/consult.pdf (Accessed 19 October 2004)

Ratcliffe, R. with Griffin, J. (1999) *Through Other Eyes: how the world sees the United Kingdom.* London: British Council http://www.britishcouncil.org/work/survey/mori1_2.pdf (Accessed 19 October 2004)

Ratcliffe, R. (2000) *Through Other Eyes 2: how the world sees the United Kingdom* http://www.britishcouncil.org/work/survey/toe2_1.pdf (Accessed 19 October 2004)

Richardson, R. (2002) *Recognising Diversity: representations of UK society, creativity and learning in the work of the British Council. An evaluation.* London: British Council. http://www.britishcouncil.org/diversity/download/mso186_.doc (Accessed 19 October 2004)

Richardson, R. and Miles, B. (2003) *Equality Stories: recognition, respect and raising achievement.* Stoke-on-Trent: Trentham.

Runnymede Trust (2000) *The Future of Multi-Ethnic Britain: the Parekh report.* London: Profile Books.

Taylor, C. (1992) *Multiculturalism and the Politics of Recognition.* Princeton, NJ: Princeton University Press.

Part Two
Teachers Talking Citizenship

4

Teaching for a better world: language education in Japan

Kip Cates

Language teachers at the beginning of the twenty-first century live in critical times. Our world faces serious issues of terrorism, ethnic conflict, social inequality and environmental destruction. How can we prepare our students to cope with these challenges? What is our responsibility as language teachers in a world of war, poverty, prejudice and pollution? What have global issues got to do with foreign language education, anyway? Isn't our job just to teach grammar, vocabulary and communication skills?

Responding to global concerns

There are several good reasons why foreign language educators should care about world issues. One is ethical and personal. Many language teachers find it morally wrong to stick their heads into their textbooks and pretend these problems don't exist. Another reason concerns the aspirations we have to be a language teaching profession. The idea that the professions have a moral responsibility to society in the practice of their specialised skills goes back to the Hippocratic Oath in ancient Greece, where doctors swore to use their professional skills for the good of society. The past 20 years have seen a rapid increase in the number of professional groups working to solve world problems through research, education and action. Two such groups in the field of medicine are Physicians for Social Responsibility and the 1985 Nobel Peace Prize winner International Physicians for the Prevention of Nuclear War. Similar groups exist for scientists, lawyers, psychologists and professionals in other fields. If language teachers truly aspire to be a profession in the real sense of the word, then they must consider this aspect of social responsibility.

Teachers have a professional responsibility to promote justice and peace in the world and this is affirmed by numerous international organisations, including the United Nations and teacher trade unions. One of the most influential policy documents in this respect is the 1974 UNESCO *Recommendation Concerning Education for International Understanding, Cooperation and Peace*. This calls for a global perspective at all levels of education, understanding and respect for other cultures, an awareness of the rights of individuals and groups, and a readiness on the part of the individual to participate in solving the problems of his or her community, nation and the world at large (UNESCO, 1974).

Another reason for dealing with global issues in language teaching concerns our status within the field of education. The education profession has always recognised its unique responsibility in promoting peace, justice and an active concern for the world's problems. Education International, the world federation of teachers' unions that was created in 1993 from the merger of The World Confederation of Organisations of the Teaching Profession (WCOTP) with the International Federation of Free Teacher Unions (IFFTU), has as one of its main aims:

> to promote for all peoples and in all nations peace, democracy, social justice and equality; to promote the application of the Universal Declaration of Human Rights through the development of education and of collective strength of teachers and education employees. (Education International, 1993)

This continues the tradition established by its precursor (WCOTP, 1989).

The American organisation, Educators for Social Responsibility (ESR), was set up in 1982 and one of its priorities is to help educators 'respond effectively to local, national, and international crises related to interpersonal and systemic violence, intolerance, and global conflicts and war.' (ESR, 2004). It is one amongst many organisations with similar aims that can be found across the world.

For language teachers, the most significant attempt to relate their professional concerns and world issues is UNESCO's Linguapax project. The name Linguapax comes from the Latin words *lingua* (language) and *pax* (peace) and refers to a series of seminars dealing with language teaching for international understanding. The first Linguapax conference, held in Kiev, in

1987, brought together such groups as the International Association of Applied Linguistics (AILA), the International Association for the Development of Cross-Cultural Communication (AIMAV) and the World Federation of Modern Language Associations (FIPLA) to discuss the 'content and methods of teaching foreign languages and literature for peace and international understanding'. The resulting Linguapax Kiev Declaration made four specific recommendations to foreign language teachers:

■ to be aware of their responsibility to further international understanding through their teaching

■ to increase language teaching effectiveness so as to enhance mutual respect, peaceful co-existence and co-operation among nations

■ to exploit extra curricular activities such as pen-pal programmes, video exchanges and overseas excursions to develop international understanding

■ to lay the basis for international co-operation through classroom co-operation using language teaching approaches responsive to students' interests and needs.

(UNESCO, 1987)

The Declaration also called for UNESCO and its member nations:

■ to take steps to inform students and their families of the potential of foreign languages to promote better knowledge of world issues and concerns

■ to organise workshops for foreign language teachers and students on contemporary world issues of direct relevance and interest to young people, such as environmental protection and the struggle against poverty and hunger.

(UNESCO, 1987)

Views of language educators

A number of leaders within the English language teaching (ELT) profession have addressed the importance of global education for teachers of English as a second language (ESL) and English as a foreign language (EFL). Some stress how global issues can provide meaningful content for language classes. Others stress the mission language teachers have to teach for a better world. Alan Maley, for instance, argues that a global education approach to English language teaching would bridge the gap between the classroom and real life:

> Global issues are real: the spoilation of the rainforests, the thinning of the ozone layer, acid rain, nuclear waste, population growth, the spread of AIDS, state violence and genocide in Kurdistan, Tibet and Bosnia, ecological disaster and war in Ethiopia and Somalia... the list is depressingly long. What has this to do with the teaching of EFL? English language teaching has been bedevilled with three perennial problems: the gulf between classroom activities and real life; the separation of ELT from mainstream educational ideas; the lack of a content as its subject matter. By making global issues a central core of EFL, these problems would be to some extent resolved. (Maley, 1992: 73)

Speaking at the start of the 1990s Brown, whose principles for language teaching inform many language teaching courses, said:

> Global, peace and environmental issues intrinsically affect every human being on earth. These issues provide content for your content-based humanised ESL teaching of the 90s. We teachers have a mission, a mission of helping everyone in this world communicate with each other to prevent the global disaster ahead. The 90s are in your hands. (Brown, 1990)

The idea that foreign language teaching can contribute to creating a better world is not new, of course. Indeed, much traditional language teaching makes vague references to global education ideals. However, as one noted language educator points out, this has mostly remained wishful thinking:

> It may be well to ask ourselves whether international understanding, let alone world peace, can be said to have been promoted by the considerable amount of foreign language teaching in the world. Diligent learning of foreign words and phrases, laborious copying and recitation of irregular verb paradigms, and the earnest deciphering of texts in the foreign language can hardly be considered powerful devices for the development of international understanding and good will. (Rivers, 1968: 262)

In other words, teaching grammar and language structures is not enough. If our language students are truly to become socially responsible world citizens, then global issues and the four goals of global education (global knowledge, skills, attitudes and action) must appear explicitly in our language teaching curricula.

Global issues in the language classroom

There are a variety of ways in which EFL teachers in Japan are working to integrate global issues and global education into their teaching. These involve language teaching content, methods, materials, course design, teacher training and extra curricular activities.

Content

Language teachers have a degree of topic flexibility that other subjects do not. It is not surprising, then, that content is one area of teaching where instructors are attempting to integrate a global perspective. This approach is described by one Japan-based language educator as follows:

> 'Global issues' and 'global education' are hot new buzzwords in the language teaching world. Global education is the process of introducing students to world issues, providing them with relevant information and developing the skills they will need to help work towards solutions. Those who support global education usually defend it in this way: we all need to use reading passages, dialogues and discussions in our teaching, so why not design these with content that informs students of important world issues and challenges them to consider solutions? (Provo, 1993)

Global issues can be addressed even when students are just starting to learn the sounds of a foreign language. One example is the Japanese junior high school text Cosmos English Course (Oura *et al.*, 1989: 5) which teaches the English sound /p/ by using the word 'peace'. Grammar, usually felt by students to be the dullest area of language study, can also be taught with a global perspective through a change of content. Starkey (1988), for example, describes how teaching past, present and future tenses becomes more meaningful when students study the past, present and future of global issues. This can involve students in studying the historical background of an issue such as environmental pollution, looking at the present situation of pollution in their community or country, then doing future-oriented activities concerned with solving this problem. Comparatives can similarly be practiced through comparing human rights in different countries or through contrasting global inequalities of First World wealth and Third World poverty. Some teachers have designed exercises to teach students the conditional 'if...then' while promoting environmental awareness. These revolve around pattern practice based on model sentences such as 'If we recycled paper, we'd save more trees' or 'If we all picked up litter at our university, we'd have a beautiful, clean campus' (Hockman *et al.*, 1991).

The four language skills of reading, writing, listening and speaking can also be integrated with global issues content. One British teacher, for example, has based a complete English 4-skills lesson on the international human rights organisation Amnesty International (Sandilands, 1989: 22). This begins with students *listening* to information about Amnesty International, *speaking* their opinions concerning human rights, *reading* about the work of Amnesty International in its English newsletter, and then *writing* English letters calling for the release of prisoners of conscience around the world.

Teaching Methods

Global education is as much a matter of how we teach as of what we teach. For many teachers, this involves a shift from passive to active learning, from teacher-centred to student-centred classes, from language-as-structure to language-for-communication-about-the-world. This shift in teaching method often stimulates teachers to experiment with new approaches such as experiential learning. This can lead to trying out class simulations and role plays which get students out of their seats and actively involved in exploring global issues in the foreign language. Role play can be adapted to almost any situation. I am aware of students practising foreign language skills in scenarios based on: civil rights organisations in the Southern States of the USA and their opponents; logging companies and tribal peoples in a tropical rainforest; acting as UN ambassadors in a model United Nations simulation.

Other teachers try to bring the world into the classroom by inviting to class guest speakers, such as visitors from other parts of the world or representatives from groups such as Greenpeace. By offering opportunities to debate with the visitors, teachers promote communicative English skills as well as interest in world cultures and global issues. Yet other teachers attempt to develop global awareness and language skills through student projects such as social issue interview surveys or class presentations on organisations such as UNICEF and Oxfam.

Materials

A global education approach to language teaching requires that teaching materials impart the knowledge, skills and attitudes required to help language students become socially-responsible world citizens. In many textbooks, however, world issues are conspicuous by their absence. Even when textbooks do touch upon global issues, they often tend to treat them trivially as an overlay on the linguistic syllabus. A number of commentators criticise the 'tourist-consumer' flavour of many language texts, with their focus on shopping, travel and fashion. Ironically, far from promoting intercultural understanding, it is the case that: 'foreign language textbooks provide fertile grounds for discovering bias, racism and stereotype' (Starkey 1988: 239).

Whilst stereotypes remain an issue in language textbooks, at least a number of foreign language textbooks now include lessons dealing with global themes. A look at EFL school textbooks in Asia will turn up global issue language lessons that include topics such as Martin Luther King, tropical rainforests, Mother Teresa and world hunger. A number of commercially-published English language textbooks appeared in the 1990s dealing specifically with global issue themes. The titles give a good indication of the content of these publications: *Making Peace* (Brooks and Fox, 1995), *Global Views* (Sokolik, 1993), *The Global Classroom* (de Cou-Landberg, 1994), *Environmental Issues* (Peaty, 1995), *Earthwatch* (Stempleski, 1994), *Impact Issues* (Day and Yamanaka, 1998) and *The World Around Us* (Hoppenrath and Royal, 1997).

Classroom language teachers unable to find the global teaching materials they want often write their own language lessons on topics as diverse as refugees, recycling and world religions. Yet others design teaching materials around the many exciting global education textbooks, teaching packs, CD-Roms and videos now available in the US and UK from a variety of global education resource organisations (see the list at the end of this article).

Course design

A growing number of language teachers in Japan are experimenting with global education approaches to course design. One approach is to design content-based language courses around the topic of global issues such as peace, human rights and the environment. Another approach to designing courses on English for world citizenship is to focus on the area of world themes. This involves integrating the presentation and practice of language skills through topics such as world religions, world flags and world languages aimed at promoting global awareness and international understanding. The rationale for this has been explained as follows:

> Teaching (world) cultures by themes gives students a more complete picture of what cultures are, helps them make productive comparisons, and shows how we share basic aspects of living that each culture expresses in a different way. (Kepler, 1996: 3)

Not much work has been done to develop entire courses or materials in this area, though some writers have included a world themes approach or component in their EFL texts. Examples include *Speaking Globally* (Grohe and Root, 1996), *The Global Classroom* (de Cou-Landberg, 1994) and *Go Global* (Tokiwamatsu, 1998).

For the past several years, I have experimented in my Japanese university EFL classes with this kind of international themework aimed at practicing language skills while promoting global awareness and world citizenship. The one-semester, four-skills course I've designed includes the following themes:

- ■ World Names
- ■ World Languages
- ■ World Newspapers
- ■ World Place Names
- ■ World Writing Systems
- ■ World Music
- ■ World Religions
- ■ World Gestures
- ■ World Festivals
- ■ World Money
- ■ World Flags
- ■ World Education

Each 90-minute lesson has two sets of aims – a set of language learning aims and a set of global education aims. Language learning aims revolve around vocabulary expansion, four skills development, oral fluency and communicative practice. Global education aims revolve around acquiring knowledge of world themes and skills for world citizenship. I will explain how this works in practice.

For our lesson on world names, students read about naming customs from places such as England, Korea and West Africa, write explanations of their own Japanese names in English and learn to identify people's ethnic origins from first and last names. At the end of the class, students have not only improved their English but have acquired a very basic know-how about names that may help them to be culturally sensitive world citizens. For example they learn that last names ending in *-escu* are Romanian, that the suffix *-opoulos* is common in Greek names and that the name Lagstrom is likely to indicate a Scandinavian background.

For the class on world religions, students master vocabulary, strengthen language skills, and develop fluency as they acquire a basic understanding of world religions, a knowledge of their history and traditions, respect for the beliefs of others, and an interest in the world's faiths. Students start with a vocabulary game, working in groups to fill in a chart with the English names of the founder, god, believer, holy book, place of worship and holidays for five major world religions: Christianity, Islam, Judaism, Buddhism and Hinduism. They next read capsule profiles of these religions, then reinforce their knowledge through oral comprehension questions. The lesson finishes with a world religion quiz and a class discussion about religion and students' lives.

The lesson on world flags has students read about the power and meaning of flags, study the designs of 180+ flags of the world, listen to the stories behind individual flag designs and learn to recognise common world flags. For homework, students research one nation's flag or design a world flag and explain its meaning.

The lesson on world money introduces students to the history of money, to currencies around the world and to the symbols found on money. They then do a money analysis game where they learn to infer cultural information about countries such as Vietnam, Egypt, Russia and Thailand by analysing images on actual banknotes from these nations.

For the lesson on world writing systems, students study the history and features of 10 world alphabets and learn to identify on sight scripts such as Russian cyrillic, Korean hangul and Hindi devanagari. As homework, they research and try actually writing alphabets such as Arabic, Thai or Egyptian hieroglyphics and write an English report about the experience.

For the class on world languages, they study about language families, then read basic information (history, number of speakers, places spoken, unique features) about seven world languages: Arabic, Chinese, French, German, Korean, Russian and Spanish. After analysing tape-recorded examples of these languages being spoken, students are given a language recognition quiz to see if they can identify the language from the sound alone. They then practice basic conversational expressions (Hello, How are you?, Fine, Thank you, My name is..., Good-bye) in all seven languages until they can greet each other in simple Spanish or hold a short conversation in Chinese. As homework, they research a particular language or try out their new conversational ability in seven languages on the foreign students at our university and describe their experience in English.

All these topics are studied in English and students work hard to acquire the vocabulary, grammar and language skills for each theme. At the same time, they come away from each class with a greater awareness of world cultures, a deeper knowledge of topics such as world religions and with world citizen skills such as the ability to identify world flags, world languages or world writing systems.

Extra curricular activities

Extra curricular activities offer another way for language teachers to combine global issues with the study of foreign languages. Some language colleges in Japan, for example, hold annual International Awareness Seminars as part of their autumn school festivals. These seminars feature English speech contests on global themes or English-speaking guest lecturers from groups such as UNESCO or Friends of the Earth.

Out-of-class volunteer activities comprise another area where language teachers are helping to internationalise their students. As one Japan-based teacher puts it:

> volunteer work with global issues can be a perfect context for teacher-student contact outside class. Personally, because I'm committed to a just world free of war, hunger and poverty, and because I'm committed to my students learning English, I find there's no better combination than working on global issues with students outside the classroom. While students get the language practice that I need them to get to complement my classes, we are working together for the future world of our choice. (Bamford, 1990: 35)

One out-of-class activity carried out by Bamford is a charity walk in Tokyo where students and teachers practise English while walking 35 kilometres to raise money to help end world hunger.

Overseas school tours are a further way to promote international under-standing among language learners. Many schools in Japan, for example, send groups of students abroad for summer language practice and overseas home stay programmes. Though these undoubtedly promote students' language ability and intercultural awareness, such visits centre on countries like the USA, tend to focus on Disneyland and other tourist sights, and sometimes involve more shopping than intercultural understanding. A number of lan-guage educators in Japan, in contrast, are increasingly trying to awaken the interest of Japanese students to other areas of the world (Hinkelman, 1993). One college English teacher in Tokyo, for example, regularly leads English school trips to India, where her Japanese students stay with Indian families and learn about life, culture and social issues in India. Another teacher has taken Japanese students to the Philippines to help them improve their English as they learn about problems and issues facing developing nations. Another English teacher took her Japanese high school girls to Korea to visit their Korean sister school. Since English was the only common language between the Korean and Japanese girls, her students came home with improved English skills as well as a greater understanding of Korea, its people, the sad history of Japan's colonial occupation of Korea and the need to work for better relations between the two countries.

Teacher Training

Teacher training is another area of language education where interesting global education initiatives are taking place. One such initiative is an inten-sive summer workshop run by the Language Institute of Japan (LIOJ) for high school English teachers. This brings together classroom English teachers from Japan and from countries throughout Asia who study together to improve their teaching methodology and language skills while using English to explore topics involving education, culture and social issues.

Another initiative is a graduate-level English teacher training course entitled 'Global Issues and Cooperative Learning'. This is offered by Teachers College, Columbia University of New York at its Tokyo campus as part of its international MA-in-TESOL programme. The course, to which I contribute, gives graduate students in the field of English language teaching the chance to explore teaching ideas, resources and activities from fields such as global education, peace education, human rights education and environmental education. These teachers then go on to practice designing and teaching model English language lessons on global education themes for use in their own schools.

The Global Issues in Language Education Special Interest Group (GILE SIG)

One organisation actively involved in promoting global education among language teachers in Asia is the Global Issues in Language Education Special Interest Group (GILE SIG) of the Japan Association for Language Teaching (JALT). This group aims to promote global awareness, international understanding, and the study of world problems through language education. Its members comprise classroom teachers, school directors, publishers and textbook writers who share a special interest in global education and its aims of enabling students to effectively acquire a foreign language while empowering them with the knowledge, skills and commitment required by world citizens for the solution of global problems. The Global Issues SIG thus has a double commitment to excellence in language education and to teaching for a better world.

GILE SIG was officially established in June 1991 and since then has engaged in research, education and action. Its aims are:

- to promote the integration of global issues, global awareness and social responsibility into foreign language teaching
- to promote networking and mutual support among educators dealing with global issues in language teaching
- to promote awareness among language teachers of important developments in global education and the related fields of environmental education, human rights education, peace education and development education.

GILE SIG members receive the Global Issues in Language Education News-letter, a 24-page quarterly newsletter packed with up-to-date news on global education and foreign language teaching. Each issue contains a wealth of information such as: suggestions for teaching about human rights; reports on international pen pal programmes; notes on the latest peace education books; global awareness teaching activities for tomorrow's class. Regular features include summaries of articles on global issue themes from language teaching journals, profiles of global education organisations, global education book reviews and a networking section where language teachers can write in to share information about topics such as teaching about world hunger or to get information about things such as recycled paper for classroom handouts.

GILE SIG members benefit from the group's networking contacts in Japan and abroad. These range from Japanese development education groups to the Tokyo office of Amnesty International, from the international English teachers' group TESOLers for Social Responsibility to the European LINGUAPAX movement, and from advocacy groups such as Oxfam and Save The Children to world bodies such as the United Nations, UNESCO and UNICEF.

A major activity of the GILE SIG is organising presentations on global education for local, national and international language teaching con-ferences. Recent sessions held at the annual international conference of JALT have included colloquia on peace education and language teaching, panel discussions on teaching global issues through English in Asia, workshops on designing socially-responsible language teaching materials, seminars on environmentally-friendly language teaching, and an annual global education materials display exhibiting resource books on global education and human rights education for language teachers.

GILE SIG also runs a number of projects. These include the publication of special magazine issues on global education, the production of English textbooks on global issue themes, the donation of used EFL textbooks to countries such as Vietnam and Kazakhstan, fund-raising for projects such as children's homes in India, the promotion among language teachers and students of international events such as Human Rights Day (10 December) and the creation of a website featuring back issues of the GILE Newsletter (www.jalt.org/global/).

GILE SIG also brings to Japan experts in global education for national work-shops, lectures and conferences to introduce foreign language teachers to teaching methods and materials linked to global issues. These have included

Japan lecture tours by Russian peace educators, by Australian conflict resolution experts, by environmental education experts from Canada and Singapore, and by European Linguapax experts from Germany and Spain.

Conclusion

We can summarise the benefits of teaching about global issues, international topics and world cultures in an English as a foreign language class. One benefit concerns relevance, excitement and student motivation. The countries, themes and issues taught each morning in an English for world citizenship class appear each night on the TV news. There is an immediate and daily lesson in relevance. The knowledge about world nations, topics and issues, and the ability to discuss these in English, translates into an empowering feeling for students of becoming international cosmopolitans. All this leads to a degree of student excitement and interest that is hard to compare to more traditional language classes.

A second benefit is the promotion of international understanding. Japanese students often have little incentive to meet foreign people or adequate world knowledge to interact effectively with them. Some feel they know nothing about foreign countries or global issues, and so have little motivation to talk about them. Others, more proficient in English, may try to strike up conversations but end up angering foreign visitors. Linguistic proficiency, after all, has no inherent relation with international understanding. It doesn't matter how good your English is (or your intentions are), for example, if you risk alienating fellow students because you are unaware of the possibility that they observe dietary traditions associated with their religion or that they may be fasting.

Once students have studied world cultures, world themes and world issues in English, however, they have a sound base of knowledge and awareness from which to expand. A direct result is the warm response of foreign people to meeting Japanese youth who know something of their countries and world issues, and who can communicate this in English. This not only leads to friendlier relations between individuals (and increased English use), but improves the reputation of Japan as an outward-looking nation where people are interested in and knowledgeable about other countries, cultures and concerns.

By designing language learning activities, materials and curricula around global issues, world themes and international understanding, English language teachers can truly contribute to promoting world citizenship. When done effectively, this can lead both to improved language proficiency and to the development of global knowledge and skills. The final result is the development in students of the philosophy attributed to Thomas Paine: 'The world is my country, all men are my brothers, to do good is my religion'.

References

Bamford, J. (1990) Education and action beyond the classroom, *The Language Teacher* 14 (5): 35-37. (JALT, Japan).

Brooks, E. and Fox, L. (1995) *Making Peace*. New York: St. Martins Press.

Brown, H.D. (1990) *On Track to Century 21*. Plenary talk at TESOL'90, San Francisco, USA.

Day, R. and Yamanaka, J. (1998) *Impact Issues*. Hong Kong: Lingual House/Longman.

de Cou-Landberg, M. (1994) *The Global Classroom*. Reading, MA: Addison-Wesley.

Education International (1993) *Aims and Principles*. Brussels: EI http://www.ei-ie.org/main/english/index.html (accessed 14 October 2004)

Educators for Social Responsibility (2004) *Mission Statement*. Cambridge, MA: ESR http://www.esrnational.org/aboutesr.htm (accessed 14 October 2004)

Grohe, W. and Root, C. (1996) *Speaking Globally*. New York: Prentice Hall Regents.

Hinkelman, D. (1993) Overseas tours to research social issues, *The Language Teacher* 17 (5): 5-10. (JALT, Japan).

Hockman, B., Lee-Fong, K., and Lew, E. (1991) *ESL: Earth Saving Language*. Workshop given at the March 1991 TESOL Convention, New York, USA.

Hoppenrath, C. and Royal, W. (1997) *The World Around Us: social issues for ESL students*. Toronto: Harcourt Brace.

Kepler, P. (1996) *Windows to the World: themes for cross-cultural understanding*. New York: Doubleday Books.

Maley, A. (1992) Global issues in ELT, *Practical English Teaching*, 13 (2): 73.

Oura, A. *et al.* (1989) *Cosmos English Course*. Tokyo: Sanyusha Press.

Peaty, D. (1995) *Environmental Issues*. Tokyo: Macmillan.

Provo, J. (1993) Teaching world issues, *Daily Yomiuri Newspaper*. 18 March, Tokyo, Japan.

Rivers, W. (1968) *Teaching Foreign Language Skills*. Chicago: University of Chicago Press.

Sandilands, B. (1989) From listening to letter-writing, *Practical English Teaching,* 10 (2): 22-23.

Sokolik, M. (1993) *Global Views: reading about world issues*. Boston: Heinle and Heinle.

Starkey, H. (1988) Foreign languages in: G Pike and D. Selby, *Global Teacher, Global Learner*. London: Hodder and Stoughton.

Stempleski, S. (1994) *Earthwatch*. New Jersey: Prentice Hall.

Tokiwamatsu Gakuen. (1998) *Go Global: a global education resource book for language teachers*. Tokyo: Kagensha Press.

UNESCO. (1974) *Recommendation Concerning Education for International Understanding, Cooperation and Peace*. Paris: UNESCO.

UNESCO. (1987) *Linguapax Kiev Declaration on Content and Methods that could Contribute in the Teaching of Foreign Languages and Literacy to International Understanding and Peace*. Paris: UNESCO.

World Confederation of Organisations of the Teaching Profession (WCOTP). (1989) *WCOTP Handbook*. Morges, Switzerland: World Confederation of Organisations of the Teaching Profession.

Relevant websites

Social Studies School Service (USA) <www.socialstudies.com>

Worldaware (UK) <www.worldaware.org.uk>

Global Issues in Language Education Special Interest Group (Japan)
<www.jalt.org/global/sig>

Global Issues in Language Education Newsletter (Japan) <www.jalt.org/global/>

Global Issues MA-in-TESOL Course (Tokyo)
<www.tc.japan.edu/courses/method/AandHL4168.html>

5

Multilingual primary schools in Argentina

Teresa Cañas Davis

In Argentina, the private sector has traditionally responded to the challenge of educating students for a globalised world by teaching foreign languages, so as to improve co-operation and communication and avoid isolation. The number of private educational institutions dedicated to the teaching of foreign languages has multiplied in recent years. The public sector, by contrast, has not been able to provide intensive foreign language teaching. The Federal Law of Education 1992 made it obligatory to include English in the primary school curriculum as from Year 4, but this requirement was, in practice, difficult to realise. In 2001, a multilingual primary schools programme was created by the Secretariat of Education of the Government of the City of Buenos Aires (GCBA), with the aim of providing quality foreign language education to children who would not otherwise have access to it.

Buenos Aires is the capital city of Argentina. Some three million people live within the city boundaries and a further nine million in the Greater Buenos Aires area, outside GCBA jurisdiction. The city has a significant influence over the wider Greater Buenos Aires region, the most densely populated in the country, with a significant number of children from the region attending school in the city and families coming to the city to seek hospital care. Since the 1980s, there has also been steady migration to the city, some coming from Argentina's poorer provinces and the majority coming from neighbouring Bolivia, Chile, Paraguay, Peru and Uruguay, looking for work. Many of

75

the newcomers live a precarious existence in the periphery in high-rise flats or in informal settlements, while others inhabit derelict houses in the middle of the city. This is, in fact, the population which the multilingual primary schools programme is designed to serve.

Multilingual primary schools programme

In line with its policy of equity in the provision of quality education, GCBA initiated the multilingual primary schools programme in 2001. The programme introduced a second language (English, French, Italian or Portuguese[1]) into the curriculum of state-run primary schools, beginning in Year 1 (six-year-olds) and adding, in 2004, a third language from Year 4 (nine-year-olds). With the incorporation of a second foreign language, the programme is fully implemented, with 70 teachers and nine co-ordinators working in 22 of the city's 450 schools, one per school district, and reaching some 3,000 students. The programme operates in full-time schools, targeting children from disadvantaged backgrounds, and the extra teaching hours are found by extending the school day into what is generally considered to be an over-long after-lunch break.

The City of Buenos Aires is recognised nationwide as a model for curriculum design and education planning. The Secretariat of Education works steadily but slowly under the weight of this responsibility, yet administrators are sometimes obliged to rush through procedures in order to implement a project of interest to politicians in the ruling group. This was the case with the multilingual primary schools programme, which was proposed by the candidate-elect for leadership of the city in November 2000. The project had to begin in March 2001, with just a four-month lead-in period. The academic year in most provinces in Argentina runs from March to December, with a short winter holiday in mid-July and a long summer holiday commencing just before Christmas. The design therefore had to be completed in a matter of weeks, so that it could be presented in outline to the first twelve schools involved in phase one of the programme before the summer holidays began at the end of December 2000.

Rationale

The implementation of the programme is based on the belief that learning languages other than the mother tongue highlights two relevant elements in the primary school curriculum: instrumental and formative values. Instrumentally, the students learn in the same way that they learn how to become competent readers, listeners, speakers and writers in their mother tongue. They learn how to seek and elaborate information, how to become critical readers of the press, how to write a persuasive letter and to enjoy listening to a story. Foreign language learning is also a formative process: it undermines the ethnocentric illusion that there exists only one point of view, as students discover that there are other ways of signifying. People who have not had access to multicultural experiences tend to believe that their view of the world is universally valid.

A large number of people fear that the introduction of a foreign language at an early age will hinder mother tongue learning. However, much research carried out in numerous international contexts demonstrates that the teaching of more than one language strengthens mother-tongue learning, and also generates beneficial linguistic, cognitive and socio-cultural results. Among the linguistic benefits is the facilitation of metalinguistic reflection about the ways different languages function, establishing similarities and dissimilarities. Within the multilingual primary schools programme, this has been of particular importance in the case of children whose family context does not encourage the development of communication skills in the mother tongue. It was therefore critical to ensure, from the beginning, that students were provided with plenty of opportunities to understand and produce in the foreign language, drawing on a range of paralinguistic elements, such as gestures, concrete materials, songs, games and dramatisation.

The short-term objective in the early stages of the programme was to develop basic interpersonal communication skills within the school context. In time, children who have acquired these skills will be better prepared to handle written and oral texts without any paralinguistic support. They will consequently be better placed to achieve academically across the curriculum, whether they are using their mother tongue or a foreign language.

Learning other languages contributes to the development of thinking skills and enables creative and original approaches to problem-solving. Research has shown that children who know other languages are better prepared to act creatively to find new meanings and uses for everyday objects.

Finally, and importantly, language learning not only increases children's capacity to communicate with members of other cultures but also to understand and value different customs and worldviews. It increases their awareness of diversity while, at the same time, reinforcing their own identities. Knowledge of other languages and cultures appears to encourage critical awareness of one's own culture, enabling students to question common assumptions and to challenge prejudice and stereotyping.

To allow extensive exposure to the language with plenty of opportunities to develop these competences, it was necessary to allocate a significant number of school hours to the programme. The goal is to permit the transfer of sound learning strategies to later learning. It is also important that schools ensure that the teaching methods adopted in the foreign language classroom are also applied in mother tongue teaching, since knowledge of a language means being able to apply it in the social practices of comprehension and production, that is, through reading, listening, writing and speaking.

The programme is based on the understanding that it is part of a long-term policy of development and social inclusion. Given appropriate school conditions, children from economically deprived backgrounds will be better placed to acquire the tools that will help them overcome their socio-economic conditions and provide access to better personal, working and social opportunities. In other words, the multilingual primary schools programme is concerned with strengthening children's rights.

Implementation

To achieve these aims and objectives, the implementation of the programme had to be systematic, intensive and gradual, using competent teachers and appropriate assessment techniques. The programme was formally introduced in the primary school curricula from Year 1, with six teaching hours per week by qualified teachers of foreign languages. Provision was also made to employ an assistant teacher for every two classes whenever these had more than 25 students. As the programme developed these assistants helped students who joined the schools with no knowledge of the foreign language. In this respect they play a key role, since there is a relatively high degree of mobility among the student population of many schools in the programme, and in the public educational system a school which has vacant places must accept anyone who applies.

As members of the team who had designed the original foreign languages curriculum for the City of Buenos Aires City (unique in the whole country) and members of the new task force, we were charged with the responsibility of adapting the curriculum to meet the new needs of the multilingual primary schools programme and finding teachers to implement it during the summer recess. The old curriculum had been designed with just two to three hours per week of foreign language teaching in primary and secondary schools. The new programme, which required six hours' teaching time, required class teachers, schools and principals to adjust their timetables and adapt to completely new conditions.

As overall coordinators we were extremely fortunate to be able to bring together a highly committed team of school coordinators, which meant it was possible to address the challenging task of dealing with the concerns of those who were employed in the existing foreign language supervising structure. Not surprisingly, many of the existing personnel were suspicious of the new programme and resisted its introduction. One of the most difficult obstacles was that of recruiting suitably qualified teachers of English, Portuguese and Italian, since we found ourselves in direct competition with the private sector, where highly skilled teachers such as those we were seeking can command much better salaries and working conditions. For example, although we managed to secure well-prepared teachers of French for the first two years, we started experiencing greater problems in 2003.

The materials needed to provide the print-rich environment and the class textbooks we required posed an obstacle beyond the resources allocated to state schools. This is a particular challenge in serving the needs of an economically deprived school population in a critical economic situation, such as Argentina has experienced since the year 2000.

It was at this stage that the representatives of foreign countries whose languages were taught came to the rescue in many different ways. In the case of English, the British Council provided textbooks for each child, readers for the classroom libraries, teaching materials and arranged visits by specialists in early years education to provide support in continuing professional development and the initial training of teachers. The support given by the Teacher Assistance Programme (TAP) was also of great value. TAP works through the British Council to link British university students with local authorities in a range of countries. The students work as assistants, supporting teachers of English and receiving a salary from the local authorities. An interesting contribution has been the offer to send teachers already working in the programme for a short visit abroad to become directly acquainted with the culture of the country. The aim is to provide an incentive to join the multilingual primary schools programme, making the idea of teaching a foreign language in a public sector school more attractive.

One of the most interesting features of the programme is the engagement of the team of school coordinators, all of whom are established specialists in foreign language teaching, in designing innovative assessment and evaluation processes. The main responsibility of the school co-ordinators, apart from regular visits to the schools, is that of organising weekly meetings with the teachers they supervise, so as to encourage reflection and collaborative lesson planning. At these meetings, groups of teachers exchange their experiences. All meetings take place on the same day of the week so as to allow for the possibility of bringing teachers of different languages to meet together on a regular basis to discuss in a genuinely multilingual situation. Meetings also provide a positive framework for teachers to explore differences and similarities between languages, concepts which can be communicated to the children. One interesting development has been the proposal by the foreign language teachers to devote one meeting per month to working collaboratively with their class teacher in developing language-teaching activities.

Outcomes

Towards the end of the second year, we undertook research to support the introduction of the second foreign language and to measure the extent to which participation in the programme hindered or enhanced children's learning of their mother tongue. Interviews with Year 2 students (aged 7 years) revealed a surprising degree of metalinguistic reflection in both the foreign language and the mother tongue. Children made reference to spelling differences and lexical comparisons. The findings were confirmed by teachers and parents in separate interviews. Most important was the involvement shown by parents in their children's learning. Class teachers reported that parents, who had previously appeared indifferent to school practices, were now beginning to question the teaching methods they used.

The multilingual primary schools programme, which was initiated in response to a specific social need as perceived by politicians, has had to come face-to-face with a whole range of issues of importance to the teaching profession, including those relating to identity, diversity and citizenship. It has generated and brought to the surface wider discussions and debates about a more general need to reform teaching methodologies. These debates have had an impact on teacher education programmes in the City of Buenos Aires. They have pushed the teacher education institutions to take steps to reconsider the relationship between theory and practice in their programmes and to place greater emphasis on the need to introduce trainee teachers to school classrooms at an earlier stage in their education.

Bibliography

Abdadallah-Pretceille, M. (1996) *Education et Communication Interculturelle.* Paris: Presses Universitaires de France.

Abdadallah-Pretceille, M. (1996) Competence culturelle, competence interculturelle, *Le Français dans le Monde: recherches et applications. Cultures, culture*: 28-38.

Abdadallah-Pretceille, M. (1999) Ethique de l'altérité, *Le Français dans le Monde: recherches et applications. Enjeux et interrogations.*

Auge, M. (1997) *Pour une Anthropologie des Mondes Contemporains*. Paris: Flammarion.

Cummins, J. (1981) *Bilingualism and Minority Children*. Ontario: Ontario Institute for Studies in Education.

Cummins, J. (1984) *Bilingualism and Special Education: issues in assessment and pedagogy*. San Diego, CA: College-Hill.

Curtain, H. and Pesola, C. A. (1995) *Language and Children: foreign language instruction for an early start*. Harlow: Longman.

Ellis, R. (1994) *The Study of Second Language Acquisition*. Oxford: Oxford University Press.

Garabedian, M., Barbe, C. and Garabedian, J. D. (1999) Pourquoi commencer plus tôt l'apprentisage des langues? *Cahiers du Centre Interdisciplinaire des Sciences du Langage*, 14, Université de Mons.

Long, M. (1984) Instructed interlanguage development, in L. Beebe (ed.) *Issues in Second Language Acquisition: multiple perspectives*. New York: Newbury House.

Preston, D. (1989) *Sociolinguistics and Second Language Acquisition*. Oxford: Blackwell.

Revuz, C. (1998) A lingua estrangeira entre o desejo de um outro lugar e o risco do exilio, *Lingua (gem) e Indentidade*. Campinas: Mercado de Letras. Translated from French original in Education Permanente (1992) 107.

Richard-Amato, P. (1989) *Making it Happen*. Harlow: Longman.

Note

1 It is hoped that German will also be included at some stage.

6

Reclaiming the right to question: language teachers in Brazil

Vanessa Andreotti

This paper examines a curriculum project which was part of a larger capacity building programme for English language teachers in the State of Paraná, in southern Brazil. The project was a site of a critical pedagogical experience centred on the themes of agency, difference and citizenship. The capacity building programme involved more than 2000 public sector teachers and ran from December 1999 to December 2002. It was owned by the State Secretariat for Education of Paraná, funded by the World Bank, managed by the British Council and delivered through a local network of private and public sector institutions. The curriculum project described here took place from October 2001 to December 2002 within the stage of 'sustainability and participation' of the model for professional development of the Paraná English Language Teaching (ELT) programme.

Setting the scene

As the author of this paper, I feel the need to locate myself in the context outlined above. From February 2000 to October 2002 I worked as a consultant on the programme and was responsible for the design and implementation of various courses and activities. These included the co-development of the professional model of teacher education adopted in the second phase of the programme and the design and co-ordination of the curriculum project. The design of the professional education model and the inclusion of the stage of 'sustainability and participation' were prompted by an evaluation of the first stage of the programme. An examination of the teachers' personal accounts of the impact of the first phase courses on their pedagogical practices and personal and professional lives suggested that there was a growth of elitism and fragmentation within their communities. This conclusion was supported by my own observation that there was no common vision or agreement on priorities shared by the different stakeholders in the programme (local universities, the British Council, the government, the World Bank, the teachers). For instance, there were different perceptions as to the ownership of the process and outcomes. In particular, there was contestation over the power dynamics implicit in a programme described in terms of donors and recipients of funding and expertise. My analysis is written from my perspective as a former insider in the ELT community of Paraná. I was in a position of privilege within the programme. At the time of writing I am an insider/outsider in the same community, having kept links, but been geographically displaced.

The original aim of the curriculum project was to draw up a curricular framework for English language teaching in Paraná. The project had two main objectives in relation to teachers' professional development:

■ to give this group of teachers a 'voice' in the programme so that they could participate in the decision-making processes related to in-service education and curricular change

■ to help these teachers work as a catalyst of change in the wider community, and promote a notion of identity and participation that would be essential for the continuity and sustainability of their professional development once the initial project funding ended.

The curriculum project consisted of three phases. In the first phase, a group of 40 teachers from around the State met for two 20-hour workshops in October and November 2001. The agenda was to discuss their experiences of English language teaching and the support and outcomes they would ideally like. In the second phase, 25 of the teachers met for fifteen consecutive days in a training complex in the countryside of Paraná in January 2002. On this occasion they discussed how their own context related to broader aims of education, particularly those expressed in the guidelines of the National Parameters for Education in Brazil.

The second phase was a distance course on curriculum development designed by two local universities in partnership with the project co-ordinator which was offered to the participants in phase one. The third phase was a series of seminars held from July to November 2002, at which more than 200 educators, including teachers, trainers, policy makers and academics, met to discuss the objectives for English Language Education in the context of public sector schools of *Ensino Fundamental e Médio* in the State of Paraná. I will now examine each of the three phases and explore some of the lessons learned from each stage and from the overall process.

Phase one: giving the teachers a voice

The first activities prompted participants to think about their involvement, relationships, communication and objectives within the group. I used a participatory process and we explored group dynamics using drama and role play. At a very early stage I became aware that participants' motivation in the programme related to the personal benefits they might get from it. They hoped that the process would empower them in the competitive struggle for legitimisation and status in their own communities. Statements made by the teachers confirmed this perception. I have clustered opinions taken from my session notes, which, in my view, reflected the dominant culture of the group at that stage. The participants said, in essence:

> We are here because we are trying to teach English in the 'right' way and need to develop a curriculum so that what we do will be recognised. After the implementation of the new methodology, the students seem to be enjoying the classes more, however they do not seem to be learning much. They are not really interested in the content and do not seem to understand the importance of English to their lives, nor do the other teachers and most heads of schools, who usually say the students learn nothing in English classes. A curricular proposal for the State could solve that. It could also force the teachers of English who do not want to develop professionally to 'catch up' with us or leave.

The group was invited to explore this issue further and to list the problems of their reality in relation to English language teaching. They produced the following list:

- lack of resources (books and computers)
- low proficiency of other teachers of English in their schools
- high number of students in the classroom
- very limited number of contact hours
- low profile of the subject
- lack of awareness by heads, teachers of other subjects and students of the great importance of English for the employment market
- the isolation and stigmatisation of the teachers of English in their school communities.

When prompted to construct collectively a vision of the ideal context for language learning, the participants presented an image of a private language institute in which the students would 'have the same opportunities as the rich students to be able to speak fluent English'. Ideally they considered that the outcome of 200 hours of tuition for their students would be the ability to communicate fluently with foreigners, for example to: give directions, order food, talk about the weather, about likes and dislikes, about their city, understand song lyrics, read texts and write letters (survival English).

The participants did not question at this stage whether what was being taught in the courses in the programme was suitable for their contexts. Nor did they wonder whether the students' lack of motivation was linked to the fact that, with the exception of Foz do Iguacu (a border city), the probability of communicating in English with foreigners was extremely low. That is to say that there was little likelihood of them ever using English for survival, whether in their regions or abroad.

However, they did start to think in political terms, realising that they would need the support of a big constituency to lobby the government for the improvements they sought. This caused them to start to perceive the fragmented community as a disadvantage. Another crucial common perception that this process induced was the hierarchical gap between local universities and the practitioners. The great majority of participants criticised their pre-service teacher training (delivered as an undergraduate course) and blamed the local universities and their tutors for their pedagogical and linguistic deficiencies. Their perception was that what came from abroad was of better quality than local provision. Their perceptions echoed the assumptions of the then State Secretary for Education.

The participants then decided to design a questionnaire for parents, students, headteachers and teachers of other subjects. They wanted to enquire about their perceptions of the objectives of learning English. The design of the questionnaire reflected the teachers' assumptions about the importance of English for the job market as the main justification for ELT. This conforms to the discourse of the government and the World Bank and reflects the content of the courses and materials being used in the programme. The main justification for learning English, implicit in the questionnaires and in the voices of the teachers themselves, was that globalisation had made English a universal language that would give the students access to information and access to a 'higher culture' and to possibilities for class mobility.

Phase two: unpacking what was said

The curriculum project group spent fifteen days together advancing the discussions about the curricular proposal while another 200 teachers of English were doing an immersion course focusing on language skills, sharing the same venue. It was expected that one of the outcomes of the curriculum discussions would be an outline of the content of the curricular proposal for the State. The curriculum project participants provided daily workshops for the teachers in the language course in an attempt to promote participation and teacher empowerment by displacing the notion of the trainer.

Whilst planning the activities for this phase, I received the compilation of responses to the questionnaire designed by the teachers in phase one. Forty schools in the State had completed the form. The results confirmed the participants' perception that the guiding principle for English in the curriculum was about preparing students for the market, and this made me feel very uncomfortable.

Now that I had empirical evidence to confirm the conclusions of the group, I started questioning where the assumptions behind the English for the market principle came from and where this process was leading to. I also began to question my own idea of empowering the teachers by opening up a space where their voices could be heard and their authentic knowledge valued. Where did this knowledge come from? How was it constructed? What are the implications of taking the lead from the teachers? Were there any contradictions in relation to what the group intended to achieve and what was possible to achieve?

When thinking about education in a context of poverty, it is useful to think about some of the difficult options educators need to face, such as:

- ignoring the context and providing standard education, hoping that it will work the same way as it does in other social classes

- setting out to rescue the most able students in that context to provide opportunities for class mobility

- intervening in the context to promote improvements and change by bringing in models and strategies developed by experts

- working with the community in establishing what kind of education is needed in that context.

In this case, there was an overlap of aspects of the four options above. The teachers wanted to give the students the same kind of education the middle and upper classes have access to. They wanted to provide the best students with opportunities for class mobility. They thought that would happen by bringing in a methodology that was developed by 'experts' which would work in any context. And they had decided to consult the community in order to confirm and legitimise their decisions, which were based on the idea of globalisation and the necessity to adapt to the economic world order.

Nevertheless, in a country like Brazil, with striking levels of inequality, the assumption that the sole purpose of education was to empower students to become better players in the economic system contained contradictions. The notion that education increases competitiveness, assumes that poverty is merely a deficit of knowledge. It ignores the fact that precisely this competitive system that is being strengthened by education, may in fact also be generating inequality and poverty. Given that unemployment levels are rising both in developed and developing countries even for the social subgroup that is considered highly qualified, I concluded that selling the English language as a commodity that would bring status, open the doors of the market and provide higher wages, was like selling an illusion for the vast majority of students in public sector schools in Brazil.

Moreover, the justifications for learning English presented, particularly the unexamined assumptions about globalisation, have serious implications in relation to assumptions of agency (as a capacity to intervene in the world) and alterity (how individuals construct and relate to difference), as well as for society. This is an example of ideological reproduction through education, as extensively explored by sociologists (Young, 1971; Giroux, 1992; Bourdieu and Passeron, 1994). These assumptions shape an adaptive conception of human agency, reproducing the perception of a pre-determined scale of social progression and an 'upward linear path of development easily conflated with notions of modernisation and westernisation' (Pennycook, 1999). These factors in turn shape power relations on the basis of what is considered higher or lower in this linear path. This adaptive conception of agency prevented teachers from perceiving any change in their vision of different possible realities other than in terms of economic success. As a result, I realised that if we were to attempt to challenge these conceptualisations of agency and alterity in order to create the conditions in the group for better informed decisions, the notion of English for the market would need to be critically examined.

On the first day of the second phase I shared with the group some of my thoughts about the possible contradictions mentioned above. I proposed that we should choose from two possible options in deciding how to use the rest of our time. We could either carry on and discuss the content for a curriculum based on the assumptions already defined, or we could place the assumptions under scrutiny and explore their origins and implications in educational, economic and social terms. This idea of looking into the past to re-evaluate where we are coming from in order better to understand the present and the potential for the future has been coined 'unlearning', by Gayatri Spivak (1996 and 1999). This concept is central to her wider project of a post-colonial pedagogy (Landry and MacLean, 1996).

Although they recognised that if the second option was chosen the outcomes of the discussions were unpredictable, the majority of the group still voted for it. Consequently, for the following fourteen days our process of 'un-learning' started as we tried to trace the origins and implications of the dominant educational discourses. We did this by using the knowledge of the participants and Freircan rhetoric on citizenship education. The discussions took place in a 'safe house', which has been defined as:

> social and intellectual spaces where groups can constitute themselves as horizontal, homogeneous, sovereign communities with high degrees of trust, shared understandings, and temporary protection from legacies of oppression. (Pratt, 1991:40)

However, our safe house was neither homogeneous nor as free from internal conflicts as Pratt suggests

The participants in the curriculum programme were aware of the elitism generated by the hierarchies created around levels of English proficiency and teaching competence. This was reinforced by their daily contact with the teachers on the language course. Together, these factors helped them to perceive the contradictions in their original visions of an ideal reality, as generated in the first phase of the project. In the safe house the process of un-learning soon became a process of individual and collective self-examination, in which the agonistic and antagonistic relational process of construction of our (multiple) identities became evident and our subjectivities, privileges and aspirations were brought under scrutiny. This self-critical approach was useful for creating new forms of agency and it prompted the group to name itself 'the Pathmakers', inspired by the saying:

> The future is not some place we are going to, but one we are creating. The pathways towards it are not found, but made. The making of those pathways changes both the makers and the destination. (Schaar, un-dated)

There were a number of outcomes to this second phase. The group began to question their representation on the steering committee and the principles underlying the committee's decisions and its courses, activities and policies. The general feeling was that sustainable change could not happen from the top down, but that it would require the involvement of the wider community. Furthermore, the participants' motivation was now based on the difference they could make to other people in their contexts, as opposed to the personal advantage motif expressed in phase one. In relation to the curricular proposal, they decided that new principles for the curriculum needed to be found, and more time was necessary to reflect on the issue. As one of the participants put it: 'We now know what we don't want, but we are not ready yet to define what we do want'. Another asked: 'Do we have the legitimacy to define a curriculum proposal? Shouldn't the other teachers be involved in this discussion?'

By the end of the second phase, the group had two priorities. First they wished to continue their discussions from the point at which they had left off. Secondly, they hoped to extend the opportunities for discussing the aims and objectives to more teachers and other members of the ELT community in the State. To achieve this a partnership between two universities and the project co-ordinator was formed for the design and delivery of a distance course on curriculum theory and development, which provided opportunities for further discussions about the curriculum. However, the difficulty in measuring the outcomes and the apparently subversive character of the new directions for teacher participation established in this phase were seen as problematic by some of the stakeholders (although celebrated by others). The extension of opportunities for other teachers did not happen until the third phase of the project.

Phase three: an expanded 'safe house'

For the third phase, a series of three short courses or seminars were planned to enable discussions about the principles for English language education in the State. The seminars were intended to involve the wider community. They were open to other teachers and included local academics, trainers, policy makers and critical outsiders. Academics from other States working in the area of critical theory and pedagogy were invited as contributors to help spark the discussions. The seminars covered themes such as critical pedagogy, citizenship, post-modernism, post-colonialism, English as a lingua franca and intercultural communication (Canagarajah, 1999). A report was written for each seminar, which had from 150 to 200 participants and which involved between fifteen and thirty hours of presentations and discussion.

The central purpose of the seminars was to raise the participants' awareness of the implications of globalisation processes for their local educational, economic and social contexts. In particular the seminars explored ways in which language education could intervene in this process and affect some of its consequences. Participants were encouraged to think in terms of the development of critical agency, defined by Spivak (1996: 294) as 'accountable reason'. They also started to define citizenship in its most robust sense, as opposed to global economic citizenship (Spivak 1999: 400).

In Figure 6.1, I have tried to represent some of the questions raised, the inherent complexity of the issues discussed and the interdisciplinary nature of the process which blurred the boundaries between politics, philosophy, education and linguistics as a mind map.

The main anxiety in relation to the questions addressed was the re-definition of the justifications for teaching English once the English for the market principle had been deconstructed. The greatest fear was the possibility of not finding any other reason for teaching English in public sector schools in Paraná. This led some participants to question and resist the 'unlearning' approach. However, there was also a strong feeling that, in the current world order, English proficiency has an important role in providing the tools for talking back and in reclaiming agency as the right to co-write history.

In my view, the difficulties and anxieties experienced by the teachers were primarily related to the articulation of these new justifications, an exercise that had not been attempted by that community before. By the time I left the programme, I had the impression that the participants had indeed started down a new pathway. Although nobody could tell where it was leading to, the process of construction had the potential to continue to change both the makers and the destination if the safe house or an open space for awareness raising and discussions was secured.

However, the Paraná ELT programme came to an end the following academic year, when a new State government took over and suspended its contract. The new government decided not to provide any in-service education specifically for language teachers. The only opportunities for professional development remaining for the teachers of English, apart from a few universities that continue to offer in-service education programmes, are those offered by the British Council or the American Embassy. I cannot evaluate at this stage the impact of the project in the general ELT culture of the State or predict its long-term repercussions in the smaller communities that have been affected by people who took part in it. What I can say is that the outcomes of the

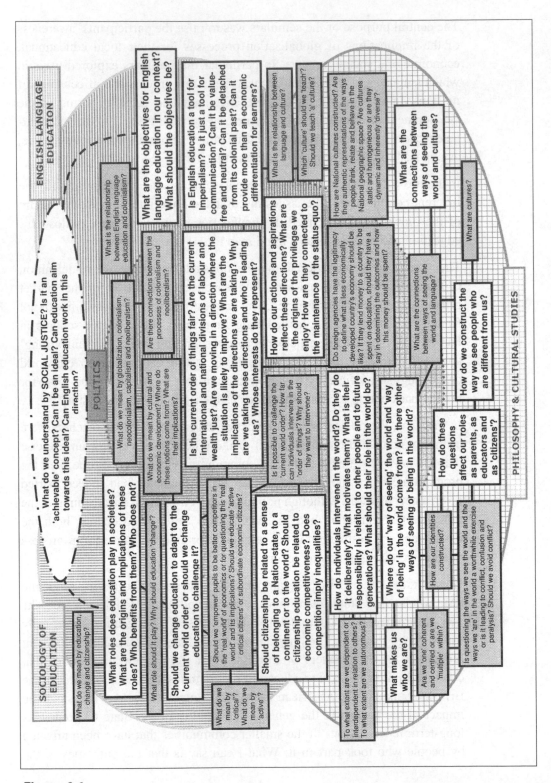

Figure 6.1

second and third phases of the curriculum project did deeply affect the course of events in the last year of the capacity building programme. This was achieved by creating a space where difficult and complex questions could emerge and be addressed, relatively unaffected by institutional powers. However, it remains to be seen whether this space will ever be re-created within the context of Paraná.

References

Bourdieu, P. and Passeron, J.-C. (1994) *Reproduction in Education, Society and Culture.* London: Sage.

Canagarajah, A. (1999) *Resisting Linguistic Imperialism in English Teaching.* New York: Oxford University Press.

Giroux, H. (1992) *Border Crossings: cultural workers and the politics of education.* New York: Routledge.

Landry, D. and MacLean, G. (eds.) (1996) *The Spivak Reader.* New York: Routledge.

Pennycook, A. (1999) Development, culture and language: ethical concerns in a postcolonial world, in J. Shaw, D. Lubelska and M. Noullet (eds.) *Partnership and Interaction: proceedings of the fourth international conference on language and development.* Pathum Thani: Asian Institute of Technology.

Pratt, M. (1991) *Arts of the Contract Zone.* New York: MLA.

Schaar, J. quotation found on The Quotations Page http://www.quotationspage.com/ (accessed 7 October 2004)

Spivak, G. (1996). Subaltern talk: interview with the editors, in G. MacLean, and D. Landry (eds.) *The Spivak Reader.* New York: Routledge.

Spivak, G (1999) *A Critique of Postcolonial Reason.* Cambridge, M.A. and London: Harvard University Press.

Young, M. (1971) *Knowledge and Power.* London: Collier-Macmillan.

51

7

Interdisciplinary and humanistic learning:
a case study from Cuba

Dolores Corona

Introduction

In light of the ongoing processes of globalisation, language education in Cuba is being considered from a new perspective. Our concept of building citizenship is closely related to the continuing expansion of the population's cultural horizons, as a means of both personal and societal growth. Language education is valued as one of the key elements in the enhancement of cultural and educational development and thus it is considered as a component of citizenship education. Within this context, aims and contents of language syllabi are changing so as to contribute to the empowerment of citizens and the greater integration of Cuba in the concert of nations. With these changes, an effort is also being made to strike a proper balance between the defence and promotion of our national language and cultural identity, on the one hand, and the development and promotion of the learning of foreign languages and cultures and universal values, on the other.

Given the reaffirmed status of English as Cuba's first foreign language, this case study will illustrate some of the main changes taking place in English language teaching (ELT) in the training of professionals in Cuban universities. Basically, such changes consist in moving from courses centered on reading within the boundaries of professional fields to integrated courses with an interdisciplinary, inter/multicultural, and humanistic approach. Some lessons learned during the implementation of these changes are discussed and future actions are identified.

ELT in Cuban universities

Since the mid 1980s, most Cuban universities have been implementing a Reading English Across the Curriculum Programme (REACP), pairing English professors with content-area instructors in a joint effort to get students to read for information in English in academic problem-solving activities beyond the walls of the language classroom. Systematic external evaluations of this programme conducted from 1997-2000 showed that most of our senior undergraduate students were capable of drawing out relevant information published in English about their professional fields.

Nonetheless, language education policy-makers, university administrators and teachers of English at the tertiary level were not satisfied. With the turn of the century, such good results were coming in too late; a reading capacity in English was not enough. Our courses, centred on reading within the boundaries of the professional fields, were no longer relevant either to individual or societal interests and needs. It became evident that our undergraduates, i.e. the new generation of Cuban professionals, needed a renovated language education, one which could help them to successfully meet the demands and challenges of a changing world, one that promotes more exchanges, more mobility, more joint ventures as well as the increasing use of information and communication technologies. In addition, research and development increasingly follow an inter-disciplinary approach, so our English for Specific Purposes (ESP) courses were also in need of revision.

Innovations

In our view, globalisation is not to be seen as a one-way process in which some people are only 'receivers' and 'consumers' of information, while others are the 'producers' and 'providers' of information. We believe that a truly effective and beneficial globalisation implies a two-way process, a process characterised by equal opportunities to have access to knowledge and to contribute to its development. Such a two-way process would be also characterised by mutual respect and better understanding among the parties, so that everyone's culture is validated and everyone's voice is heard.

Since 1999, Cuban universities have been making changes in their language syllabi to equip undergraduates with the communicative skills required to enable them to participate effectively in different forms of exchange and interaction. In addition, efforts are being made to follow an inter/multicultural and humanistic approach in our classes. In our approach we aim at devising task-based activities to foster links between the professional fields and the world of art, literature, and the social sciences. In doing this, we are providing our students with opportunities to expand culture and to reflect on their views and their reality, and to compare and contrast them with those of others, in the hope of contributing to their full-fledged development.

It is evident that moving from courses centred on reading within the boundaries of the professional fields to integrated courses with an interdisciplinary, inter/multicultural, and humanistic approach is a huge challenge for Cuban English language professionals. This effort is all the more challenging because our day-to-day linguistic environment does not offer many opportunities to practice English – or any other foreign language – outside formal language learning settings. Therefore, we have been experimentally working on creating opportunities across the curriculum to develop communicative skills in English.

Within this context, I would like now to comment briefly on two crosscurricular workshops I conducted with third-year undergraduate students at the School of Sociology at the University of Havana, which were developed as complementary activities to courses in Sociology of Knowledge and Women's Studies. Following the advice of the content-area instructor, students were given an article published in an American magazine comparing the roles of and changes experienced by women in the USA in the 1970s and the 1990s. In the first workshop, the students read the material and made comments about the most striking changes, and briefly pointed out some similarities with and differences from the experiences of Cuban women in the same period. (Occasional use of Spanish was not penalised). Then we negotiated the content of the follow-up workshop. Students agreed to form teams to collect more information about Cuban women. In addition, they agreed to prepare a formal oral presentation of their findings, and to roleplay in a simulation activity as Sociology undergraduate students taking part in an international symposium in which English was the official working language. They were given two weeks to prepare. Both the content-area instructor and the present author coached and acted as resource persons for their presentations. The content-area professor also provided specialised counselling.

In the second workshop, we conducted the simulation activity with good results. The group was made up of nineteen students (fourteen women and five men). All of them were between 19 and 20 years old. I observed more similarities than differences in their analyses and responses to the tasks given. Both men and women reacted positively, and they shared many opinions. Any disagreements were as likely to be between women students as between the men and the women. Women in the group expressed different points of view and the debate did not polarise between men and women. Students collected data that allowed them to show advances in Cuba concerning women's status. For example, in the field of higher education, they presented information related to the percentage of female university graduates. Cuban women represented 37 per cent of university graduates in the academic year 1976-77 and by 1996-97 the percentage had increased to 57 per cent overall, with 59 per cent in Economics and 55 per cent in Social Sciences and Humanities. Indeed, in some fields it was already over 60 per cent (Medical Doctors 65 per cent and Natural and Exact Sciences 64 per cent). Despite improvement in all fields, several students pointed out that some areas are still dominated by men. They then went on to discuss possible causes and reasons for this. In addition, they were proud to talk about gender equity attained in Cuba concerning equal pay for equal work. Students were really surprised to learn that, according to the magazine, in 1978 women full-professors in the USA earned 91 per cent of the salary earned by their male counterparts, and that in 1997 this had fallen to 88 per cent. On the other hand they discovered that although by the 1990s, Cuban women represented more than 63 per cent of the entire professional and technical labour force in the country, in leading positions it was only around 39 per cent.

Twelve out of the nineteen students who participated made their presentations with no errors or with minor structural and pronunciation mistakes which did not affect intelligibility. From the instructional point of view, it was more semi-controlled practice than creative practice, since to a great extent students followed the format, vocabulary, and syntax of the original article. In this respect, it was a first step in integrating reading with speaking and writing. But from an emotional and attitudinal point of view, we believe we made considerable progress. Students proved to themselves that they could cross the border of 'receiving and understanding information' and travel towards the region of 'providing information and making themselves understood'. Their self-esteem was increased. They were proud of being capable of talking about advances and achievements made by Cuban society in relation to women's empowerment and equality, and also about aspects of the lives of women that still need improvement. Moreover, when asked about the preparation for the workshop, students pointed out that team work for the purpose of producing an 'international performance' about Cuba enhanced both their capacity to work together to reach a common goal and also developed individual responsibility. That is, it promoted interdependence, and, because each student had a personal duty to reach the common goal, self-reliance.

As for myself and the content-area instructor who worked with me, we felt that we had also taken a step forward towards helping our students to cope more effectively with what our society expects from its professionals and also with their own personal expectations and life goals. As educators we also experienced satisfaction with the success of these cross-curricular activities because we attested the potential of an integrated, interdisciplinary, inter/ multicultural, and humanistic approach to language learning for the training and moulding of better professionals and better citizens. While improving their English competence, the students became involved in the analysis and discussion of a crucial social issue world-wide. Learning how other people were doing in this area expanded their knowledge about other cultures and triggered their interest in learning more about the Cuban experience. Working in teams fostered co-operation and solidarity among the members of the group. Talking about Cuba contributed to strengthening their sense of nationhood. Furthermore, thinking of 'the other' while preparing and making their presentations provided opportunities for sharing.

Reflections and evaluation

It should be noted, however, that some problems were also faced during the implementation of the experience. Seven students out of nineteen could not cope with the language challenges of the second workshop. When analysing their performance it became clear, with hindsight, that these students should have been given the opportunity and the alternative of participating as observers until they were ready to participate as presenters. Had such opportunity been given to them, they would have received more individual attention and they would have moved at their own pace without experiencing high levels of stress. They would have had more controlled practice with the material of the first workshop, before moving to collecting and providing new information.

Another lesson learned was that simulation activities and team-teaching were effective in paving the way to the implementation of the new approach, with most students reacting in a positive way to role-play. Nonetheless, we also concluded that more efforts have to be made to work with the students in preparation for real exchanges, taking advantage of the increasing number of collaborative projects between Cuban universities and those from the English-speaking world. We believe that much can still be attained in language education if students have opportunities to experience real communicative situations where their Cuban and Latin American voices can be heard through a foreign language of wide international communication, such as English.

Other programmes are being devised to apply this approach to English for Science and Technology (EST) courses, linking science and technology to the humanities and the social sciences. We are also aware that we cannot neglect a current trend world-wide in ELT at university level: the growth of English for Academic Purposes (EAP). Within the Cuban university context, EAP courses have to be devised, first of all, for our teachers of English, who will in turn teach these courses not only to undergraduates, but to a significant number of our faculty as well. All the pedagogical initiatives so far implemented, and those to come, share a common goal. Their intention is to make a difference not only in instruction, but in education as well. These programmes aim to broaden the cultural horizons of our undergraduates, by giving them food for thought, for the mind and for the soul, whilst they are learning English.

Our enormous challenge is the generalisation of these changes in all undergraduate programmes nation-wide. Such generalisation demands the active and conscious participation of the entire university community, including teachers of English, content-area professors and undergraduate students. Much work still needs to be done. We have to continue working in syllabus design and in the professional development of our teachers of English to ensure the success of our new goals in ELT in universities. Most content-area professors need more training in English, with courses and activities especially tailored to improve their language competence in academic discourse. This is crucial for the implementation of an English Across the Curriculum Programme. Moreover, teachers of English and content-area professors have to develop more teamwork so as to devise cross-curricular, task-based learning activities with suitable materials in relevant topics in order to meet our ambitious new approach to language teaching.

Finally, the close relationship between language learning and citizenship education in Cuba can be illustrated by the example of a mass-audience television programme. This clearly shows the extent to which language education is gaining momentum in Cuba and that the teaching of English as well as the teaching of French, German, Italian and Portuguese have come to occupy an important place in our society. These new educational efforts represent the broadly inclusive goal of reaching all sectors of Cuban society.

A comprehensive cultural TV programme called *Universidad para Todos* (University for All), which aims at enhancing culture on a mass scale, began its daily broadcasts nation-wide early in October 2000. It consists of courses in a wide spectrum of fields and disciplines, including Spanish and foreign languages. The English language course was among the first programmes to be broadcast. It had an audience of more than one million viewers from every region of the country and from all social backgrounds. This mixed audience of different age groups had different interests and needs, and the programme makers attempt to provide material that is both entertaining and focussed.

Conclusions

In Cuba, current changes in language education are closely related to building citizenship because they are precisely aimed at preparing our people to develop their own cultural knowledge and range of references in order for them actively to participate in the development of the nation. By helping them to fulfil their personal cultural and educational goals, the nation will also benefit. Both the teaching of Spanish language and foreign languages have a broadly inclusive goal of reaching all sectors of society. Language education is valued as one of the key elements to enhance the cultural horizons of the entire population, and thus it is considered as a component of citizenship education.

Moving to integrated courses in foreign languages with an interdisciplinary, inter/multicultural, and humanistic approach is an imperative of language education in Cuban universities. Language learning can be a value-added experience when students increasingly engage in activities that foster reflective attitudes and critical thinking concerning their own share of responsibility in the attainment of personal and societal goals.

While writing this paper I recalled some words spoken in the nineteenth century by José Martí, Cuba's national hero. Martí stated: 'Trenches made of ideas are worth more than trenches made of stones'. (*Trincheras de ideas valen más que trincheras de piedras*). Reflecting on his words. I came to the conclusion that the more languages our citizens learn with an inter/multicultural and humanistic approach, the more trenches made of ideas they will have from which to cry out for a better world.

Related bibliography

Corona D. and Garcia O. (1996) English in Cuba: from the imperial design to the imperative need, in J. Fishman, A. Conrad and A. Rubal-López. (eds.) *Post-Imperial English: status change in former British and American colonies 1940-1990*. Berlin and New York: Mouton de Gruyter.

Diaz, G. (2000) Technothrillers and English for Science and Technology. *English for Specific Purposes* 19 (3): 221-236.

Guillén, C. (1992) Los aspectos socioculturales del área de lengua extranjera y el programa linguapax, *Comunicación: Lenguaje y Educación* 16: 83-91.

Hyland, K and Hamp-Lyons, L. (2002) EAP: issues and directions, *Journal of English for Academic Purposes* (1): 1-12.

8

Intercultural Learning: connecting young citizens through ICT

Tuula Penttilä

This case study describes an approach to teaching English and Swedish in an upper comprehensive school in Espoo, Finland, a city of some 200 000 inhabitants not far from Helsinki. We use ICT intensively to promote an intercultural dimension to language learning. The school has had classes with special themes like intercultural education and media and it has the ENIS (European Network of Innovative Schools) kitemark.

Context

Mankkaa School has some 330 pupils and 35 teachers. It is an upper comprehensive school for classes seven to nine, the final years of compulsory education, which is provided for ages 7-16. The foreign languages that our pupils study are English or German as the first FL, which they start in the third grade (age 9); Swedish (Finland's second official language) starting in the seventh grade (age 14); and French or German, starting in the eighth grade. The school is divided into four departments, the year groups for grades seven, eight and nine and a department of special educational needs which specialises in supporting children with autism. The school is well equipped for Information and Communications Technologies (ICT). We have about 85 computers, which are distributed around the school. There are two computer classrooms, but every classroom has at least one computer. We have a local area network, internet/ fixed light cable and video conferencing facilities. All students have their own email addresses and some classes have their own electronic portfolios on their class homepages.

In our school teachers take a class through from grade seven to grade nine so as to provide continuity and enable the learners to benefit from a long term relationship with their class teacher who gets to know the individual learners very well. This case study relates to a ninth grade group that I had been teaching since they entered the school in the seventh grade.

All our lessons are double lessons lasting 90 minutes so as to facilitate group research tasks and projects. We organise project days for our year group and since teachers tend to do most of their teaching within one grade, we can organise project work across the year group without it affecting the other departments. Our school's goal is to enable pupils to be responsible for their own development, for the atmosphere in the school, for the school building and to share a common concern for the local and global environment. We aim to provide them with skills and tools they will need in the future, particularly: knowledge about and familiarity with ICT; a commitment to ethical and moral values; and the ability to live a full life, enjoying culture and the arts and appreciating the pluralism of our world.

Curriculum

In Finland, a centralised national curriculum was replaced in the mid-1990s by the delegation of responsibility for curricula issues to local authorities and schools. This happened at a time of political and demographic change in Finland. Finnish people historically tended to perceive themselves as a rather homogenous nation, with some small minority groups like gypsies and Lapps. However, like other European countries our demographics are changing with the arrival of refugees and other migrants. These changes are particularly marked in schools. Although schools have had to develop their own curricula, they are still expected to comply with the National Framework Curriculum (National Board of Education, 1994). Amongst other objectives, this requires schools to address new areas of content and to ensure that the curriculum reflects cultural diversity. In particular there is an expectation that students will have opportunities to interact with a variety of cultural forms and traditions.

In our case, at Mankkaa School, we looked for opportunities to work on cross curricular topics, in keeping with our emphasis on project work. We found that the curriculum area of foreign languages was particularly fruitful in providing opportunities both for project work and for intercultural education. One advantage that language classes present is that there are numerous opportunities to join international projects, since language is not a barrier to communication between project organisers. Additionally, international projects provide opportunities for the learners to practise their language skills in situations of real communication.

In English, our curriculum is organised on the basis of one broad theme for each grade. They learn about the USA in the seventh grade, the United Kingdom in the eighth and as much as possible about the rest of the English speaking world in the ninth. Whenever possible we try to cover the topic in as many subjects as possible, not just during time allocated to the foreign language. The preparation of this approach is very demanding on the teachers. However, the teachers do not entirely control the process of project work and the participants carefully evaluate each project. If the project is repeated the feedback is taken into consideration.

Global Citizenship Maturity Test

In English curriculum time we offer a project course of eighteen lessons. Many of the pupils in this course have chosen to do the Global Citizenship Maturity Test organised by the Finnish United Nations Association (Finnish UNA, 2001). This certification was initiated as part of the Global Citizenship Study Programme that was started experimentally by students from Finland's UNESCO schools in 1994. The objective of the Global Citizenship Study Programme is to fulfil the educational goals of the UN, UNESCO and Finland's UNA by increasing opportunities to discuss issues of peace, development, human rights, culture, the environment, the economy and refugees. Its main objective is to encourage development towards a mature adult life and to reinforce self-directed, critical learning. The underpinning philosophy of the test is that understanding oneself and one's own culture is the basis of all learning. Students learn to recognise the responsibility of the individual and recognise opportunities to influence the world. The programme is based on UNESCO's goals for personality development and the aims are described as follows:

> The Global Citizenship Maturity Test promotes self-directed learning and international education. The emphasis is on individuality, but the project increases also the sense of community as it teaches students innovative methods of working collaboratively. It encourages the student to gather information from a varied range of sources and to use that information diversely. Self-evaluation, interactive skills and making the most of electronic databases are other important features of the test. It aims at a deeper knowledge and understanding of the world and encourages positive self-esteem. You will learn more about individual responsibility and how to make a difference. World citizenship requires your being inventive, determined, flexible and creative. It means believing in your

own abilities and having a willingness to co-operate with others. (Finnish UNA, 2001: 2-3)

The programme encourages participants to engage with many different methods of research including learning to use electronic research methods and telecommunications. It emphasises self-evaluation and assessment of one's own work as well as interaction skills. The topics vary from racism to sports, and the time to complete the test varies from three months to a number of years. The test can be done individually or with a partner, who may be from another country. The first step is for the student to register with the Finnish UNA, which offers help either electronically or in person. Each participant identifies a tutor, who may be any teacher. The research begins with the collection of articles of interest from the media until a suitable topic is identified and agreed.

The topic chosen has to be examined from as many sides as possible using libraries, field-trips, interviews and the internet. Participants keep their collected data in a folder. They also keep a personal journal for personal opinions, experiences, thoughts and questions. The end product has to include a written part, but it can also include a video, an audio-tape or multimedia. The information that has been gathered has to be usable. Participants are required to prepare a plan for the dissemination and utilisation of the research findings. For instance participants may present a paper to a class, make an exhibition, organise a theme week or a field trip, put on a play, a concert or a parents' evening at school.

Intercultural education

Young people are aware that today's world is characterised both by increasing economic and political integration and, simultaneously, by numerous conflicts between nations, cultures and ethnic groups. To be able to live in this kind of world we have to develop a new level of cultural awareness and sensitivity, an ability to understand and to communicate with persons from other cultures and nations. We need to highlight not just what is different, but equally importantly what we have in common. As foreign language teachers we have the duty to assist our learners to become citizens in a world that demands knowledge, problem-solving skills, competence and caring. We are preparing our pupils for real life; helping our students become politically and socially aware requires bringing real life into our teaching.

In preparing our learners to live in this global world, teachers have adopted a number of strategies. These are referred to by various titles depending on the context, so for instance this part of the curriculum may be called international education, education for international understanding, global education, multicultural education or multicultural studies. In spite of these different titles, they all have a common core of concern with increasing understanding and communication between culturally and ethnically diverse peoples (Tella *et al.*, 1996). My personal preference is the term intercultural education, in which the main areas of concern are: peace education, human rights education, environmental education, cultural education, development education (awareness of issues in the developing world) and media education. The basis of intercultural education is a clear sense of national identity and a healthy self-esteem. It is mainly education about values. It focuses on developing the whole personality of the pupil and therefore teachers' attitudes and values are crucial to the success of intercultural education (Killen *et al.*, 1997).

Some International Projects

Our foreign language teaching is based on project work and this involves using ICT. The school is well provided with the latest technology and the pupils use the internet for searching, storing and transferring data. ICT provides language learners with a rich variety of real-life communication tools and genuine communication contexts. In our language classes, projects vary from short projects of 20 minutes to long projects that may continue for years. I will provide examples of both short and longer projects.

A short project involved the students' accessing the United Nations website for schools (UN CyberSchoolBus: http://cyberschoolbus.un.org/index.asp). On the site they discovered that they were asked to write a poem of two lines on peace and that each school was then invited to submit one poem for inclusion in a book (United Nations, 1998). The students responded well to this suggestion and they each wrote a short poem. The poems were printed and displayed on the wall. The pupils then had to decide which one would be sent. They chose a poem that contained a four-letter word and, although I warned them that the poem might not be appreciated, I did not intervene. In fact the poem was included in the book, but it had been changed and the offending word removed. This project provided us with an excellent opportunity to discuss cultural differences and also censorship. The project did not take much time, but it made the pupils think about peace and what it means to them. It also gave them a sense of pride and of feeling part of a global community. The UN Secretary General, Kofi Annan wrote in the foreword of the book:

> Children know that peace comes from the heart; it survives in the respect we show our neighbours every day. They also know, often better

than adults that today's world is a global village and that we are all neighbours. (Annan, 1998)

One of our long projects was conducted with partner schools in Austria, England, Italy and Spain funded under the European Commission Comenius programme. The theme was 'Living in a Medieval City'. In our school we planned the work over the three years so that the first year they learnt about the past of our city Espoo, the second year focussed on the present and the third looked to the future. Each partner school had a site on its homepage where it put its products and these homepages were linked to each other. For example the pupils in each country wrote about the festivals celebrated in their country and the essays were placed on the website and made available to our partners.

The partner school in Austria organised a medieval feast with food and all kinds of performances and games. It made a significant impact on the local community. All the partners contributed something representing their national culture to the feast. The Spanish school was able to send a busload of folk dancers. Our contribution was to send table decorations, as we were not able to travel to the feast.

On another occasion, our school had a videoconference with the English partner school, learning about each other's food culture. We taught our partners how to make Karelian pasties and Finnish pulla and they taught us how to make mince pies. Another product was a calendar printed in four languages. Pupils in all the participating schools made drawings and poems that were collated by one of the partner schools and then printed. These are just a few examples of the many activities that took place during those three years. Co-operation has continued, with pupil exchanges and other activities.

By the time they reached the end of the ninth grade my class, which specialises in media, had participated in the following projects:

- Newsletter around the world, a monthly letter on a specific theme to a set of schools, co-ordinated from France.

- This is our Time, poems and drawings on peace and tolerance , co-ordinated by UNESCO.

- Multimedia Kids Forum, a platform for discussions, co-ordinated from Japan.

- Sending some basic school equipment to a school in East Timor.

■ Spring Day on 21 March 2003 organised by the EU. The pupils wrote about their ideas on the EU and its future. I asked a few partners in Latvia, Lithuania, Estonia and the Czech Republic to write about the same issues.

■ A student exchange with a school in Prague. We visited Prague in October and received the Czech students in April. They have learnt about each other's country and culture.

One of our most ambitious projects was the UNESCO Time Project 2002 on the theme of Diversity and Culture. This project, like so many of the others, was strongly based on using ICT. The co-ordinator was a teacher from Brazil. There was a platform, on which the pupils from different countries could meet each other. This was a closed working environment and each pupil had an individual password. The pupils started by introducing themselves and then choosing one of the following topics:

■ Diversity and culture

■ Diversity and sustainable tourism: the impact it has on cultural heritage

■ Diversity and society: yesterday, today and tomorrow

■ Diversity and the environment.

They sent in their first contribution and they were asked to comment on each other's texts and to discuss the issues raised. This part of the Time project did not work as well as the organisers had hoped. The greatest problem was that the discussion got started too late, because the time allocated to the project was too short. My pupils were disappointed, because they thought that they had not achieved much.

Later in the project we organised a videoconference with a Dutch school. The goal was to learn something from each other's culture, reflecting on similarities and differences and to start thinking about the value of having a cultural identity. We agreed in advance that we would focus on the following topics:

■ Do you think it is good to have your own culture and should we retain it?

■ Is your cultural identity important to you?

■ Should people from other cultures who come to live in your country give up their own cultural practices?

■ What aspects of your culture do you consider to be typical?

■ Are there regional differences? Which traditions or customs should be preserved and which should, in your opinion, disappear?

■ Do you think traditions and customs are disappearing? Is that good or not?

The success of a videoconference depends on preparing it well in advance. We discussed the topics in English, religious education and history classes and then the students chose the topic they wanted to discuss. We divided into six groups, each working on one of the topics and they came well prepared to the conference, as did the Dutch students. Not all videoconferences that I have organised have been successful, but this one was, in spite of the fact that the topics were not easy and some people doubted that 15-year-old pupils would be able to discuss them. The Netherlands seems to have a greater diversity of the population than Finland and therefore the pupils had a lot to discuss and to learn.

The Time project continued by discussing stereotypes. The discussion on this occasion was greatly improved because the co-ordinator used the feedback from the participants in the earlier discussion and created smaller discussion groups. The students also found the topic easy to approach. They started by discussing what kind of stereotypes there are about Finnish people, such as that we are the nation that is silent in five languages. From there we turned to other nations. In the discussion group they chose to work with the group of pupils from Brazil. They were asked to write what they knew about the Brazilians and the Brazilians did the same about the Finns. This provided a great deal of material to comment on and the students had to think carefully about their preconceptions. Then they chose a group from another country and followed the same procedure. By the end of the project the pupils felt they had learnt a lot from their foreign partners, and they had also learnt to understand their own culture better.

Conclusions

Students as well as teachers find working in international projects rewarding. Such projects are invariably motivating. Students quickly learn skills of networking. They learn a foreign language in a situation of real communication where they are communicating with real people about issues that interest them.

Working in projects is very demanding for the teacher. There is a temptation to try to do too many or too complicated projects. The teacher's role initially is to find a project and identify possible partners. Not all projects are successful. There are many things that can go wrong. Students do not always find the theme interesting and their motivation may decline. Every now and then a partner lets you down. In the Newsletter around the World project we were divided into groups of twelve to fourteen schools and one by one schools dropped out and at the end of the school year only three schools were left. In a big group there is always variety in commitment, but a successful project inspires one to go on working with international projects.

What are the benefits of intercultural education? One benefit concerns relevance, excitement and motivation. The countries, themes and issues discussed in the language classroom are those that are discussed on TV news and in the newspapers. The second benefit is the promotion of international understanding. Students learn to understand customs, manners, beliefs and other phenomena of different cultures and to be culturally aware.

In March 2003, at the beginning of the Iraq war, a little girl from Baghdad made the following statement in an International Education and Resource Network (IEARN) videoconference with some Japanese pupils:

> It may be our last meal tonight. You may never see me tomorrow. You may never see me smiling. If we young people connect with each other and work together, we will make a better world, won't we?

As language teachers we are builders of bridges and we can promote global citizenship. We can help our students to cross these bridges and hopefully to make a better and more peaceful world where people not only tolerate but celebrate differences.

References

Annan, K. (1998) Foreword, in *The Peace Poem*. New York: United Nations Department of Public Information.

Finnish United Nations Association (UNA) (2001) *Global Citizenship Maturity Test: a guide for students and tutors*. Helsinki: Finnish UNA. http://www.ykliitto.fi/maakansa/english.pdf (accessed 5 October 2004)

Killen R., Tella S. and Yli-Renko K. (1997) *Multicultural Education: towards social empowerment and cultural maintenance*. Turku, Finland: Faculty of Education University of Turku. Research Report 180.

National Board of Education (1994) *Framework Curriculum for the Comprehensive School*. Helsinki, Finland: National Board of Education.

Tella S., Yli-Renko K. and Mononen-Aaltonen M. (1996) *Two Cultures Coming Together. Part 1*. Helsinki, Finland: Department of Teacher Education, University of Helsinki. Research Report 155.

United Nations (1998) *The Peace Poem*. New York: United Nations Department of Public Information.

9

Human rights education in Romania: developing a textbook

Margot Brown and Ruxandra Popovici

Our textbook project started from the premise that it is vitally important for human rights education (HRE) to be part of young people's educational entitlement. If young people are not aware of their rights, they are unlikely to understand the basis of democratic citizenship. We listened to young people like the 17-year-old who told us: 'We have lots of rights but sadly I'm not familiar with them' and we sought to remedy this situation by providing a course that would be used widely in Romania. We identified opportunities to develop this project by involving specialist public sector language schools. Young people would learn about human rights and democratic citizenship through the medium of English.

We were inspired by a statement, made by Eleanor Roosevelt in a very different context and time:

> Where after all, do universal human rights begin? In small places close to home ... Unless these rights have meaning there, they have little meaning anywhere. Without concerned citizen action to uphold them close to home, we shall look in vain for progress in the larger world. (Roosevelt, 1958)

The textbook team decided that schools are 'small places close to home' and so planned to help young people in Romania both to know and be empowered to act on their human rights and the rights of others. We had the opportunity to do this in the context of the teaching of English.

Project background and objectives

At the end of the 1990s, both government and civil society in Romania recognised that Romania's transition to a fully functioning democracy required education for human rights and democratic citizenship. The government was clearly influenced by a growing awareness world-wide of the increasing importance of HRE in strengthening democratic systems and practices. The media at the time, which was in the process of consolidating its freedom of expression, was active in presenting examples of human rights infringements and in hosting debates over such issues as discrimination, freedom of expression, access to information and equal opportunities. They were supported in this by the campaigns of emerging local non-governmental organisations (NGOs).

Educating the young in the spirit and culture of human rights and responsibilities was also perceived as a priority by educationalists in the field of social studies. The study of civic culture as part of the core national curriculum for lower secondary grades was revised so as to raise awareness of human rights issues. Researchers and teachers aiming to support and update the content of this element of the curriculum produced a variety of materials. However, it was the English Language Department in the Romanian Ministry of Education that initiated a more systematic programme. The ministry proposed introducing the subject of human rights, taught in English, into the school-based curricula of intensive English and bilingual classes.

The ministry approached British Council Romania for support and guidance and the Council agreed to consider developing a HRE project. The project was seen as a continuation and strengthening of British Council Romania's experience in curriculum design, textbook writing and teacher training projects. The human rights textbook project, started in 2000, aimed to meet the needs of Romanian education as well as British Council objectives in the areas of English language teaching, education and governance.

The stated project objectives were to produce a textbook for the teaching of human rights and to train teachers to be confident and knowledgeable as the subject was introduced more widely. The programme targeted 16- to 17-year-old students and their teachers in those high schools where subjects are taught through the medium of English.

The introduction of human rights as a school subject can provide a framework for the students' understanding not only of fundamental human rights and of democracy, but also of rights and responsibilities in action in their own lives and the life of the community. Several steps need to be covered in such an educational programme:

- raising awareness of the individual's rights, responsibilities and freedoms as Romanian, European and global citizens

- developing skills and knowledge in the area of human rights and responsibilities

- developing the confidence and the skills to assert these rights and to participate actively in the development of the community.

As there was very little local expertise in the area of HRE, the decision was taken to work closely with a British consultant throughout the lifetime of the project. The consultant was to help to develop the expertise of materials writers both in the content and in the pedagogy of human rights. As well as ensuring a high standard product, the consultant was to assist in the design and delivery of a teacher-training programme.

A feasibility study was conducted to ascertain the interest in the subject, the type of materials needed and the training needs of the teachers. The response was overwhelmingly positive and, without exception, the opportunity to teach and learn about human rights was welcomed by teachers and students both in Bucharest and provincial towns.

A writing team was constituted, made up of teachers of English and social sciences and they undertook a short field trip to the UK to familiarise the group with best practice in human rights education. The programme, based in York, included workshops on human rights principles, practical classroom activities which had been found to be successful, visits to NGOs, meetings with students and teachers in a number of schools and hands on work on planning the textbook syllabus. The team was also introduced to the growing range of educational materials and studies in the field (see bibliography).

The writing team was convinced of the need to use active learning methods. The textbook encourages a participative and interactive pedagogy for a range of reasons. Human rights educators are persuaded by this approach because it contributes to a more democratic classroom, since it encourages skills of listening, negotiating, consensus building and honest debate. The focus on critical thinking and skills of analysis is also crucial to participative democracy. These are also among the skills of language teaching, and through the use of language in different contexts, underline the valuable and necessary link between human rights education and the teaching of English. However, the development of these skills is not the only reason for their use in the book. Teachers have increasingly begun to respond to their students' learning styles as part of their right to education. The 'how' of learning is as important in this context as the 'what' if we genuinely want students to fully access their education. This requires teachers to plan for a range of teaching styles which can respond to different learning needs.

As the materials were written, teachers and students in different regions of the country piloted sample units. The piloting was carefully prepared and teachers attended practical workshop sessions on human rights education to support their knowledge and understanding and to use the participative pedagogy advocated in the textbook, before using it in their classes.

After a period of intense work and continuous professional development for everyone involved, *Rights in Deed* (Carianopol *et al*., 2002) the human rights coursebook was published. It is now being used widely in schools in Romania and there has been considerable interest in the project from other countries. This suggests that the interest and need for HRE is very high on the education agenda globally and also that the issues and topics covered and the approach taken in the coursebook have wide intercultural validity.

The publication of the student's book and the teacher's notes to accompany it was followed by a series of training workshops with teachers in six different parts of the country. The design of a teacher training programme was a target of the team's work and completed the pack of materials for HRE produced as a result of the project. The training programme is a balanced approach between principles and practice of teaching human rights aspects in conjunction with English language development. Components of the training course include: teaching controversial issues, rights in conflict, solving interpersonal conflicts, mediation, peace making and taking action strategies. An active and democratic pedagogy, based on human rights principles, underpinned each of the topics covered.

Features of the textbook

Rights in Deed is the first human rights textbook in Romania and Central and Eastern Europe to be based on the Universal Declaration of Human Rights (UDHR) and the Convention on the Rights of the Child (CRC) and links articles in these two instruments with everyday life.

The book encourages a learning process that is achieved by the participation of students in group work, debates, role-play, simulation and project work activities. The inclusion of a multi-layered perspective: from the personal to local, national, European and global levels ensures the development of students' intercultural understanding.

The units of study integrate the following components in addition to promoting the development of English language skills:

- *human rights concepts* such as: identity, ethnicity, diversity, equality and discrimination, human dignity, poverty, conflict and peace.

- *human rights issues* such as: nationality versus citizenship, racism, multiple intelligences, refugees, homelessness and children's rights.

- *human rights values*

- a three dimensional approach to each topic: *rights-responsibilities-remedies*

- lower to higher order *cognitive skills*.

As a result, the human rights textbook increases the interest for education in English and enhances the teaching and learning of English as a foreign language. This interdisciplinary approach builds on the common background of the two subjects. Both language teaching and human rights education stress interactive and participative methodologies; learner autonomy; intercultural understanding and communication; cross curricular dimensions; co-operative learning; consideration of the students' different learning styles and different types of intelligences. Many common topics occur in both English language and social studies coursebooks (for example, identity, relationships, the media). Students learning about human rights in English are doubly motivated by the benefit of approaching issues that are part of their lives and of crucial importance for humankind, alongside improving their English language skills.

We conducted surveys on human rights issues as part of the project, contacting teenagers in: Croatia, Hungary, Morocco, Romania, Russia, UK and USA. The results are included in the book under the section: *Give us a voice!* This activity helps create a sense of inter-connectedness between the students' own communities and communities of the wider world.

Evaluation of the textbook

The project was about raising students' awareness and developing their understanding and commitment to act in the area of citizenship and human rights. We collected comments and feedback from the Romanian teenagers using the book. The learners' reactions were overwhelmingly positive and this suggests that the materials and the teacher training programme had an impact.

Some users acknowledged the learning that the course had produced:

> Now I know about important things happening around me – that I hadn't known before.

Others recognised the importance of the process and the new learning style:

> I think all classes should be this way in which you are able to say whatever you think.

> Learning about HR gave us the opportunity to know each other better.

Some commented on the effects of the classes:

> The human rights classes made me less selfish.

> These lessons made me understand how many prejudices I have, although I consider myself to be open-minded. The authors didn't try to protect us.

> After this lesson the others stopped calling me names, but this doesn't mean things have changed.

One student felt that opportunities for this learning should have been provided earlier:

> We are taught about these things too late – I am already 16.

We were given some indication that the programme had the support of parents:

> My parents are happy that school finally teaches us about life.

However, the course was not able to overcome the apparent cynicism of one student:

> It is easy to learn and talk about human rights, but who does anything when it comes to practice? You are no less bystanders than I have been all my life.

A few students had similar doubts and they were able to express them openly. The feedback from teachers and students is important for the team as they continue to work with teachers and students in various parts of the country.

Some lessons from the project

The project went well beyond its initial aims of writing HRE materials and training a group of teachers to become materials writers in Romania. It took on an international dimension. Encouragement and appreciation came from colleagues in different countries, together with requests for project documents, sample materials, books or requests for further details and information about the organisation of the project. Copies of the textbook have been distributed to British Council offices, human rights institutions and organisations and teachers all over the world. Members of the team have contributed to international seminars and workshops and they have acted as human rights education trainers in countries including Pakistan, Latvia, Estonia and Columbia.

We would like to identify some lessons we have learnt as a result of our textbook project. Some elements of a project are inevitably specific to the context in which it is introduced, but many are generalisable.

- The importance of the feasibility study

- The value of a locally produced textbook to integrate local needs with international developments

- The need for training in HRE for both authors and teachers

- The careful preparation of the piloting of the materials, involving both students and teachers

- Careful analysis of the students' and teachers' opinions and comments

- Co-operation across the curriculum between teachers of English and teachers of social science subjects

- A flexible structure to the textbook with a balance between core and optional aspects of the book

- Transfer of English language teaching skills to other subject areas.

As a result of the evaluation of the project we anticipate some revisions and we are also planning ways to widen the use of the book. Our hope is that HRE will become part of the curriculum in the years to come. This is likely to have an impact on the ways schools are organised, for if we truly want our students to be active in defence of their own and others' rights, then schools will be required to give them the opportunity to practise skills of participation within the school context. Education for democratic citizenship through human rights education is likely to require the development of school councils, community involvement and participatory learning activities.

Bibliography

Brand, J. (2000) *Human Rights and Wrongs*. Yeovil: GLADE Centre.

Brand, J. and Brown, M. (1999) *Human Rights*. London: Development Education Association.

Brown, M. (ed.) (1996) *Our World, Our Rights*. London: Amnesty International-UK.

Carianopol, M. *et al*. (2002) *Rights in Deed*. Bucharest: Humanitas Educational.

Development Education Journal (1998) Development Education and Human Rights. Special Edition: (2).

Flowers, N. (ed) (1998) *Human Rights Here and Now*. Minneapolis: Amnesty International-USA.

Holden, C. and Clough, N. (eds) (1998) *Education for Participation*. London: Jessica Kingsley.

Jarvis, H. and Midwinter, C. (1999) *Talking Rights: taking responsibility*. London: UNICEF.

King, D. (1998) *Children's Rights,* Manchester: Lucky Duck Publishing.

Roosevelt, E. (1958) Speech made on the Tenth Anniversary of the Universal Declaration of Human Rights at the United Nations, New York. http://www.udhr.org/history/inyour.htm accessed 8 October, 2004.

Smith, T. and Rainbow, B. (1998) *Global Citizenship Post-16*. Yeovil: GLADE Centre.

10

Task-based learning for citizenship

Christopher Palmer

In this chapter I outline the origins of task-based language learning and how this approach is ideally suited to cross-curricular work incorporating, in this case, citizenship education. I will seek to demonstrate that citizenship education can be taught through the careful selection and adaptation of appropriate tasks that can promote both effective language learning and a wider exploration of individual identity and relationships within and beyond one's own community. I conclude by looking at the design process for a maze that can address both language and citizenship.

Background

Since the 1960s there has been considerable growth in cross-curricular work particularly in the context of bilingual education. For example, in 2002, the government of Malaysia decided to make English, which is the official second language (L2), the medium of instruction for teaching mathematics and science. A debate as to whether or not to adopt a similar policy took place in Oman, and a number of other countries are likely to follow suit. It may, of course, be argued that mathematics and science have a relatively international vocabulary and that outcomes to learning tasks are predictable. To teach these subjects through the L2 is possibly considerably less problematic than for other, more open-ended disciplines.

Citizenship education (CE) is a relatively new subject on the school curriculum and there is still considerable debate as to its content and how this should be taught. Although it is frequently taught as a separate subject, a number of commentators have argued for teaching it across the curriculum and not in isolation. Indeed, in some countries it is defined as a cross-curricular subject with no independent space in the curriculum (Birzea, 2003). I am arguing in this chapter that there is one ideal context for teaching citizenship and that is the L2 classroom.

There are a number of arguments in favour of teaching citizenship through the L2. First, the framework for incorporating citizenship into the L2 curriculum already exists. For a number of years now, L2, and particularly English as a Foreign Language (EFL) and English as a Second Language (ESL) syllabuses have been adapted to meet the needs of specific user groups such as business, the medical and legal professions, tourism and academic study (Mackay and Mountford, 1978). In mainstream Second Language (SL) or bilingual education whole curricula have been built around the need to combine content teaching with a L2 medium (Cummins and Swain, 1986).

Secondly, topic-based teaching, the forerunner of task-based learning, has existed since the 1970s. Such teaching often involves role-play, simulation or project work, which are also commonly used within citizenship education. Oral and integrated skills-based tasks are based on topics, or themes, which broaden the vocabulary field and provide motivational interest according to the age and level of the learner (Candlin, 1981).

The third development that supports the case for using the L2 classroom for CE is the growth of personalisation and individualisation in learning. Personalisation stems from humanism, which was incorporated into communicative language teaching from the mid-1970s onwards (for example Moskovitz, 1978). In order to motivate students, oral activities were based on personal themes involving students' individual thoughts and interests. Although the humanistic impetus for this was based on personal development and whole-person learning, in L2 teaching this was often reduced to describing one's favourite food or deciding what sort of pet best epitomises oneself. Identifying one's rights and the meanings they have for learners might be considered a far more rewarding activity for personal development and one that would be expected in a CE programme.

Individualisation stems from the later interest in autonomous learning (for example Riley, 1985; Dickinson, 1987). In this tradition, there is an assessment of student needs and their individual learning strategies are also identified. By matching these it is possible to produce learner-centred programmes that students can access themselves in open learning centres. To use some citizenship terminology, learners are empowered to take greater responsibility for their learning.

Finally, there have been the developments in task-based learning itself. Task-based learning is defined as putting the achievement of the task before the language used to complete the task or, as it is often expressed, putting meaning before form. Prabhu (1987) has been particularly influential in advocating an activity-based syllabus based on the selection of appropriate graded tasks rather than on language forms. This strategy stems from a belief that language development is the result of natural processes. More recently connections are being made between communicative language learning and notions of integrated skills syllabuses (for example Willis, 1996).

The combination of these developments in languages for specific purposes (LSP) programmes, topic-based learning, personalisation and individualisation of language learning, along with activity and skills-based syllabuses has created a valuable platform for CE. This is not simply because the learner rather than the material has taken centre stage, but because communication, which underlines all language learning, needs both content and a reason for interacting with others about this content. Citizenship, which is both personal and controversial, relating to who we are and what our beliefs are, is ideally suited to task-based learning and the development of meaningful discourse or communication in a foreign or second language.

Working with tasks

Task-based learning contrasts with form-based learning where we learn a series of discrete language items in progressive order. It usually specifies a series of communicative tasks to be carried out in the L2. A classic definition of a communicative task is an activity:

> which involves learners in comprehending, manipulating, producing or interacting in the target language while their attention is principally focused on meaning rather than form. (Nunan, 1989)

In other words, outcomes are determined by communicative intent rather than linguistic structure. When you exchange information, tell a joke or solve a problem the goal is independent of the language used to achieve that goal. Learners are normally free to use any language they want. Different learners will use different strategies and, quite likely, different language forms to achieve successful outcomes. Language development is therefore prompted by language use.

Much research has been carried out into tasks and performance. Researchers such as Skehan and Foster (1997) found that students undertaking open-ended communicative tasks had a stronger engagement with the task itself and consequently spent longer in preparation and performed better, producing better formulated and longer examples of the language in question.

Stern (1992) produced a typography for suitable tasks. These include:

- Give and follow instructions
- Gather and exchange information
- Solve problems
- Give informal talks in the classroom
- Take part in drama and role-play activities.

Willis (1996) turned this classification into a generative pedagogic tool. In other words she provides more precise tasks that teachers can use to generate their lesson plans and sequences of work. The principle of this is that the teacher first draws up a series of topics suitable for the learners. For example, where the intention is to promote an understanding of citizenship, the topics might include the rights and the responsibilities of a citizen, diversity or inequality. It is then possible to identify a number of operations, based on the chosen topics, that are to be carried out in the target language. The operations may include:

- Listing
- Ordering and sorting
- Comparing
- Problem-solving
- Sharing personal experiences
- Creative tasks.

Willis also suggests an alternative 3-part cycle which could replace the conventional approach to the teaching of a new language. For many years it has been common for teachers to start by presenting the new language in a context. The second step is for learners to practise the target structure in a controlled way and finally to use the language more spontaneously or communicatively. This model is often referred to as Presentation, Practice, Production.

Willis's alternative model starts with the production phase, which she refers to as the task. For example learners could role-play magistrates and discuss appropriate sentencing options for criminal cases. The task would be to come to an agreement. Having reached agreement, they reflect on the task and prepare a report both on their approach to the task and also on the language they used. This is known as the planning phase. Finally, some groups or individuals present their reports orally or in writing and the teacher acts as chair, linking the various contributions and summing up. Teachers may also provide some feedback on the content or form at this stage. This alternative pedagogic sequence is known for short as Task, Planning, Report.

Designing mazes to provide tasks for language learning

Many language course books now include citizenship issues but few, with the notable exception of the Romanian human rights course book (Carianopol *et al.*, 2002) presented in this volume, address citizenship issues systematically. However, whether or not textbooks deal with issues, they can provide tasks that promote the development of citizenship skills.

One type of classroom activity that can be adapted to a task-based approach, incorporating both language development and CE, is the maze. Mazes combine problem-solving with simulation. They involve learners in understanding a problem and require them to reach consensus on a course of action. Learners have a number of options to consider and they must decide which best reflects the group's views. Their decision will lead to a further set of options, each offering a new challenge. A well-constructed maze can stimulate intense discussion, and allow students an opportunity to practice negotiation and debating skills in the L2. It is a key principle that the topic must be of interest, the options realistic and the exit solutions satisfying.

There are two main steps in planning a citizenship maze for language learning. The first is to identify the teaching objectives and parameters, while the second is to elaborate the story line.

Stage 1
i What is the topic area?
If the maze is too broad it will create too many choices and raise too many issues. It is important to balance this with providing sufficient scope for diversity and unpredictable outcomes.

ii What language skills?
Unpredictable outcomes imply unpredictable language but certain elements need to be identified in order to guarantee some language focus for the exercise. There may be occasions when oral production might be deemed a sufficient objective, but good practice normally requires a language learning task to provide an explicit set of language learning objectives, whether skills-based, form-based or strategy-based.

iii What social skills?
Amongst a range of other social skills closely linked to citizenship, mazes offer an opportunity to develop teamwork, problem-solving and building and defending arguments.

iv Time required

To get the best out of a maze, it is important to allow adequate time for completion. Frustration will set in if participants are unable to reach a satisfactory final outcome. Furthermore, the greater the emphasis on controlled uses of language, the longer it will take.

v Measurement of success

How the teacher recognises success and failure will depend on the relative importance attached to the citizenship learning goals when compared to the language learning goals. While failure in one area does not negate the value of the exercise, most teachers would expect a degree of success in both areas. Where the emphasis should lie will depend on the ultimate purpose of the language curriculum. If the objective of the L2 curriculum is simply to teach the language, then the lack of L2 use in the task would represent failure (Brumfit, 2001). However, if a key objective of language learning is to help students identify their place not only in their own society but also in the world community, then the activity may be considered successful even when there is limited use of the L2 in negotiating outcomes (Allwright, 1996).

Teachers may respond to the questions above by completing an outline planning grid. An example is shown in figure 10.1.

Planning	Item	Notes
Topic	Prejudice/bullying/discrimination, drawing on learners' own experience	Topics and situations close to a child's reality will provide motivational interest
Language Skills	Forms: Conditionals e.g. What will happen, if .., comparative forms Functions: Giving opinions, making comparisons, weighing up options	Although the development of fluency in oral communication skills is likely to be central to this task, accuracy can be developed through follow-up exercises such as in summaries of decisions taken or written reports
Social skills	Negotiating, reaching a compromise, reasoning, evaluating moral choices	These are important skills alongside the linguistic objectives
Time required	One session of at least 45 minutes	Could be extended so as to include a debriefing and feedback session
Measurement of success	Level of participation in discussions, shared decision making, recommendations for alternative paths, the completion of other endings	Use of the L2 may not be considered the primary goal in exercises of this kind where the focus is clearly on the task

Figure 10.1: Macro planning grid: the parameters

Planning	Item	Notes
Context	New child in school suffering from bullying	Age? Ethnic origin? Social background? Interests?
Location	Secondary school/ college inner city/rural	Choice of a realistic and identifiable context important
Players	Teacher, head teacher, friendly peers, bullies, parents, siblings	Players represent a range of attitudes to bullying, education and racism
Triggers	What events will trigger the decisions required? What form will the bullying take?	Can use findings and case-studies from research to create realistic situations
Decisions	How do different actors (teacher, peers, head teacher, family, outside agency) respond to peer group bullying? What levels of support and solidarity amongst peers? What if traditional sources of support do not deliver? Who to turn to? How do you balance loyalty with honesty?	Need to ensure decisions required moral judgements. Give a range of possible options
Outcomes	Positive for whom? Negative for whom? Clear or flexible? Decisive or fudged?	Same outcome from different routes or different outcomes from different routes?

Fig 10.2: Micro planning grid: the storyline

Stage 2

Having determined the key themes and language areas to be covered by the maze, the next stage is to start to flesh out the actual detail. Figure 10.2 illustrates some of the questions that the task designer will need to address.

I provide below an example of the start of a maze generated from the two planning grids. The options provided may be adapted according to the teaching objectives and the context. Further options can be suggested by learners. Indeed, outcomes can even be left open for learners to determine. This makes mazes very flexible in terms of language, task and emphasis.

A sample maze

1. You have just moved to a new country because of your father's job. He has a very important job and does not have a lot of time for you. Your mother has an illness, which tends to mean you often have to look after yourself. They have put you into a large inner-city school not far from

where you live. This is your first day and you only know two other pupils in your class because they happen to live in the same street as you. Because of your height (you are relatively short) , your skin colour and your accent you stand out. Some of the children start teasing you, calling you names and pulling your hair. You try to ignore them but you are quite upset.

Do you:

A. Go and tell your teacher. (Go to 2)

B. Try to talk to the children involved. (Go to 3)

C. Do nothing, deciding that it is your first day and it will be better in a day or so. (Go to 6)

2   You tell your teacher and s/he asks you to identify the children who are doing this so they can be punished.

Do you:

A. Agree to point out those pupils who were calling you names. (Go to 8)

B. Agree to point out which children are involved but only if the teacher promises not to take any action. (Go to 9)

C. Say you do not want him/her to do anything but thought they should know [you do not want to make a fuss]. (Go to 6)

3   You try to talk to the children who are teasing you but they just laugh and continue mocking you.

Do you:

A. Go to your teacher and tell him/her what is going on. (Go to 2)

B. Try and ignore it, hoping that things might get better if you try harder to integrate with other children. (Go to 6)

C. Talk to your class representative on a teacher-student committee that deals with matters of concern including bullying and school discipline. (Go to 4)

4   You talk to your class representative and s/he tells you that there is little that can be done because these children who are bullying you are quite dangerous and everyone is scared of them. If you upset them, you might get beaten up, s/he tells you, so it is best to ignore it.

Do you:

A. Accept this even though you are frightened and decide to keep a low profile staying away from these other kids. (Go to 6)

B. Try to persuade the class representative to support you by arguing that s/he would not like to be subjected to racist abuse of this kind, and that his/her role is defend the interests of the pupils in the class. (Go to 5)

C. Go to your class teacher and inform him/her of what is going on and how the class representative is unwilling to help in any way. (Go to 7)

5   Your class representative agrees to think about it but you are not convinced they will do anything. Meanwhile the abuse is continuing and so is your suffering. Further, you notice that not only is the abuse confined to you but the other children are also clearly scared and several take care to avoid you. It is becoming very distressing and you are desperate to do something about it but you do not know what.

Do you:

A. Try to persuade some of the other children to join you in order to get a petition together to have the head take some action. (Go to ...)

B. Do nothing because you are too scared recognising that, while things are not getting better, they are not getting worse. (Go to 6)

C. Go and talk to your teacher about the situation. (Go to 7)

6. You try to integrate but have little success. The bullies continue to mock you and the other children try to avoid you.

Do you:

A. Speak to your parents. (Go to ..)

B. Speak to the other children. (Go to ...)

C. Do nothing and pretend that nothing is wrong. (Go to ..)

7. Your teacher is supportive and tries to explain that the children are like this because they are not used to having children from other countries in their class. You felt s/he almost wanted to say 'children of a different colour'. Nevertheless, s/he will keep an eye on the situation and, if necessary,

talk to the head. This is all very distressing and unsatisfactory because you want to be accepted.

Do you:

A. Take action yourself by talking to the children who are calling you names. (Go to ..)

B. Decide that there is nothing more to be done and resolve to try to avoid trouble by keeping away from those boys/girls who are teasing you. (Go to 6)

C. Talk to other children about how you feel and try to get some support. (Go to ...)

8. You go out into the playground and point out the main culprits and the teacher calls them over to confront them. S/he asks you to confirm what you had said to them.

Do you

A. Repeat what you said, identifying who said what? (Go to ...)

B. Speak in general terms not identifying anyone but saying how much it is upsetting you to be treated like this? (Go to ...)

C. Deny that they really did anything because you think it will aggravate the situation? (Go to ..)

9. S/he agrees and you go to the window and identify those whom you feel to be teasing you the most. S/he tells you that he will speak to them but not let them know that you had spoken to him/her.

Do you:

A. Go away feeling relieved that you had spoken to someone about what has been upsetting you since you arrived. (Go to ..)

B. Go away still anxious because you do not really know the teacher that well and think that somehow the children who had been teasing you will get to know that you had been to the teacher and call you a squealer. (Go to ..)

C. Talk to your parents about this and ask for their advice. (Go to ..)

Continues....

Conclusion

Task-based learning using activities as mazes can provide contexts for meaningful language use, and simultaneously help to develop understandings of citizenship issues. The story-line of the maze invites learners to empathise with the protagonist, to consider options and dilemmas and to think through alternatives. Although the protagonist in this instance is a young person in school, the issues raised will be equally relevant to parents and teachers. In other words, adults can also gain benefit from undertaking this exercise and role-playing a young person. The maze also clearly spells out the consequences of each decision and the complexity of decision-making in social contexts. It has thus got the potential to contribute substantially both to language learning and to citizenship education.

Bibliography

Allwright, R. (1996) Social and pedagogic pressures in the language classroom: the role of socialisation in: H. Coleman (Ed.) *Society and the Language Classroom.* Cambridge: Cambridge University Press.

Birzea, C. (2003) *EDC Policies in Europe: a synthesis.* Strasbourg: Council of Europe.

Brumfit, C. (2001) *Individual Freedom in Language Teaching.* Oxford: Oxford University Press.

Candlin, C. (ed.) (1981) *The Communicative Teaching of English: principles and an exercise typology,* London: Longman.

Carianopol, M. *et al.* (2002) *Rights in Deed: human rights education.* Bucharest: British Council/Humanitas.

Cummins, J. and Swain, M. (1986) *Bilingualism in Education: aspects of theory, research and practice.* London: Longman.

Dickinson, L. (1987) *Self-instruction in Language Learning.* Cambridge: Cambridge University Press.

Mackay, R. and Mountford, A.(eds.) (1978) *English for Specific Purposes: a case study approach.* London: Longman.

Moskovitz, G. (1978) *Caring and Sharing in the Foreign Language Learning Classroom: a sourcebook on humanistic techniques.* Rowley. MS: Newbury House.

Nunan, D. (1989) *Designing Tasks for the Communicative Classroom.* Cambridge: Cambridge University Press.

Prabhu, N.S. (1987) *Second Language Pedagogy: a perspective.* Oxford: Oxford University Press.

Riley, P. (Ed.) (1985) *Discourse and Learning.* London: Longman.

Skehan, P. and Foster, P. (1997) The influence of planning and post-task activities on accuracy and complexity in task-based learning, *Language Teaching Research*, 1(3): 185-211.

Stern, H.H. (1992) *Issues and Options in Language Teaching.* Oxford: Oxford University Press.

Willis, J. (1996) *A Framework for Task-based Learning.* London: Longman.

11

Language teachers' reflections on citizenship

Telma Gimenez

C itizenship can be viewed as synonymous with participation, inclusion, and a sense of belonging. With that in mind, the organisers of the British Council seminar *Language Teaching and Citizenship Education in International Contexts* held in the UK, in 2003, decided to offer teachers in other parts of the world the possibility of joining in the discussion, even though they were not physically present at the event. A call for participation was sent out on a discussion list for teachers of English and as a result 28 teachers registered. Eight of these were from Brazil and four from India. Teachers based in several other countries were also represented, with one participant from each of the following States spread over four continents: Argentina, Bulgaria, Croatia, Egypt, Greece, Israel, Italy, Lebanon, Lithuania, Mexico, Nepal, Romania, Russia, South Korea, Tunisia, and the UK.

As the group moderator, not present at the seminar, I was responsible for co-ordinating the participants´ expressions of ideas through electronic mail and encouraging the exchange of points of view between the remote and the face-to-face participants. The variety of backgrounds and the teachers´ main interest in exchanging views with people from all over the world suggested possibilities for lively discussions. This was confirmed as more than a hundred messages were exchanged during the seminar week.

Defining citizenship in the context of language education

Citizenship is not a unitary concept (Challenger, 1998; Starkey, 2002). It has nonetheless been advocated by governments as one the main goals for contemporary education. In the context of globalisation, it has acquired a more dramatic urgency, reflected in numerous official documents and recommendations (UNESCO, 1974 and 1995; Council of Europe, 1985 and 2002). The recommendations define education for democratic citizenship and encourage teachers to incorporate a citizenship perspective into their teaching.

According to Smith (2004), citizenship is inextricably linked to discussions about curriculum objectives and he proposes a multinational curriculum to respond to future global trends, as identified by research (Parker *et al.*, 1999). In order to be able to cope with these trends citizens need to acquire skills and attitudes such as:

- ability to conceive of problems in global as well as local terms

- willingness to resolve conflict in a non-violent manner

- willingness to participate in politics at local, national and international levels

- ability to be sensitive toward and defend human rights.

This requires a curriculum centred around activities that promote those skills and attitudes, and not necessarily around topics to be included in the lessons. This was a prominent issue in our discussions.

There are four key perspectives that have been used by curriculum planners as they attempt to define citizenship and its place in the curriculum: a legal view, a communitarian view, a cultural view and a critical view (Ferreira, 1993; Severino, 1994; Alejandro 1998; Audigier, 2000). The legal perspective of citizenship concentrates on issues such as nationality, legal rights, legal awareness and civic education. It is perhaps the predominant view in schools and teachers working mainly with this perspective may feel inclined to teach about human rights in general, the rights and obligations of individuals in society, and to provide information related to the legal and the country's legal and voting systems. The communitarian view, on the other hand, focuses on moral development and responsibility, voluntarism, solidarity and the importance of belonging to a community and working towards its development. The cultural view emphasises sensitivity to otherness, respect for differences and tolerance. It stresses the development of intercultural competence to deal with the multiple demands of a world increasingly connected and diverse. The critical view tends to place higher value on education for awareness of power relations, and on individual and social agency or capacity to intervene in the world as well as political literacy (see Andreotti, this volume). It brings questions about representation and democracy and the role of citizens in making political decisions.

Similarly, Starkey (2002: 18, quoting Osler and Starkey, 1996) suggests a model in the format of a matrix that conceptualises citizenship based on structural/political as well as cultural/personal elements. The structural/political, at a minimal level, implies human rights education and at maximal level implies the good society and learning communities as the model. The cultural/personal, at minimal level implies feelings and choices and at maximal level implies action skills and training. This study was included in the recommended pre-reading for the seminar.

In order to assess the understandings of the group and to what extent they would recognise these perspectives, I sent an email to the registered remote participants a few days before the seminar started. I asked them to contribute their understandings of citizenship. This triggered an intense exchange of emails which reflected the diversity of meanings in teachers´ minds. The discussion started around definitions and questions about terminology; as the week progressed we moved on to the status of the English language today and global citizenship. Finally we exchanged views on concerns about the role of teachers and how to incorporate citizenship education in English language classes.

The comments of the remote participants were printed at the seminar and displayed for the face-to-face participants. A number of the UK-based participants then responded by email and joined the on-line debate.

Teachers' definitions of citizenship

Perhaps not surprisingly, several of the dimensions of citizenship presented earlier were mentioned by the participants. The majority made reference to the themes usually associated with discussions about citizenship, as highlighted in the following contribution:

> The concept of citizenship is not that simple. When we talk about citizenship, the idea of belonging to a political system and a nation comes to our minds – e.g. a Brazilian citizen or a British citizen. In this sense, it means having the right and the means to actively participate in the political and social life of that country. Of course this right is not taken for granted and it often needs to be conquered, so that people can really have better opportunities and live in a better society. In a

broader sense, citizenship has also to do with respect and concern for other cultures, other ways of being, for nature and natural resources, and everything that affects the lives of people on Earth, not only our specific culture. So, the idea of belonging to a wider community and being a citizen of the world is the one that appeals to me. (teacher based in Brazil)

As a language teacher, the contributor clearly finds the concept of national citizenship limiting and looks for a broader definition. The following contributor also recognises the importance of identities that include groupings wider than local and national:

To me the issue of citizenship is based on your identity within a region (primarily) and within the global context, and on your tolerance of diversity of religion, gender, class and disability. We come from a very conservative community wherein the respect of elders is an obligation, but is that enough? How do we show that we 'respect'? What of women's rights? We are brought up to feel and say we 'respect' or 'sympathise with'. To me that is not enough, citizenship is based on deeds and actions. How do I prove I am a 'good' citizen? And with the spread of globalisation, the coming generations will have many questions to answer: Am I a citizen of the world? How do I incorporate these international characteristics and definitions to my beliefs, my uniqueness as a Lebanese? These and other questions are issues that teachers and instructors will have to deal with in their future classrooms. What of the virtual classrooms which might be composed of students with diverse nationalities and background? (teacher based in Lebanon)

This moved us away from thinking about the concept in local terms only and we agreed that global citizenship does not require new definitions, although it operates at a transnational level and requires intercultural skills. One line of discussion evolved around whether new terminology was needed to encompass new understandings. One suggestion was that 'globalship' might be a better word to replace 'citizenship', and this triggered many reactions both in favour and against it:

As teachers and teacher educators we should devise a plan of action to imbibe the spirit of globalisation and globalship in the mind of the young people. The globalisation of English language has changed the old concept of 'citizenship' and as teachers of English we have a lot to contribute to the emerging global society. The new concept of citizenship which transcends the artificial boundaries of political entities will contribute immensely to the cause of world peace. (participant from India)

This somewhat idealistic contribution, was countered by a more sober appraisal of social realities.

> Whether by nature or circumstance I feel far less optimistic than some of the participants seem to be about what has been called 'globalship'. Living where I do, I see discrimination and prejudice at every possible level: of course, between the main ethnic groups, Jews and Arabs – unfortunately almost a given in Israel – but no less, and perhaps more severely in its effects, inside the ethnic groups themselves, which are far from homogenous. So Jews of 'Sephardi' [eastern, oriental, African and Asian ancestry] origin have been discriminated against by Jews of European extraction ('Ashkenazi'), Bedouin are considered 'backward' by Arabs, and, unsurprising in this traditional society, women are seen as less capable than men across the board and within these groupings. I will say at once that I am male, Jewish, educated, and very aware of being privileged. (participant from Israel)

The role of English as a *lingua franca*, with its advantages and its cultural baggage was reflected in the contributions that followed. However, the majority agreed that the English language represented an important asset for everybody, irrespective of their backgrounds. It is a possible tool in constructing new understandings of transnational and global citizenship. As a participant put it:

> English seems to meet the needs of most Croats who, coming from a small country, feel they have to learn foreign languages for personal and societal growth. English is seen as the language of technological breakthroughs, of alluring movies and specialist literature, a widely accepted lingua franca you can get by with in almost any country. (participant from Croatia)

However, the danger of English being taken without consideration of power and inequality was also introduced. While some felt that learning English is no longer questioned (as in India), others felt there was the danger of associating it with a new form of imperialism, especially in the context of the invasion of Iraq. This topic led to a discussion on the role of teachers of English in fostering citizenship education. Some of these roles involved teaching for tolerance:

> I believe that the main role of every educator is to teach to respect difference, both at the local and global level. English teachers can also contribute to the formation of a citizen's intercultural competence, which is the first step towards tolerance, provided they don't privilege a few countries (English-speaking and their own) and ignore the rest. (participant from Lithuania)

References

Alejandro, R. (1998) Models of citizenship, *Kettering Review,* Spring: 6-12.

Andreotti, V. (2005) Reclaiming the right to question: language teachers in Brazil, in: A. Osler and H. Starkey (eds.) *Citizenship and language learning: international perspectives.* Stoke-on-Trent: Trentham.

Audigier, F. (2000) *Basic Concepts and Core Competencies for Education for Democratic Citizenship* (DGIV/EDU/CIT (2000) 23). Strasbourg: Council of Europe.

Challenger, D. F. (1998) The positive potential in public life: citizenship and civic education, *Kettering Review,* Spring: 50-58.

Council of Europe (1985) Recommendation R (85) 7 of the Committee of Ministers to Member States on *Teaching and Learning about Human Rights in Schools.* Strasbourg: Council of Europe.

Council of Europe (2002) Recommendation Rec (2002)12 of the Committee of Ministers to Member States on *Education for Democratic Citizenship.* Strasbourg: Council of Europe.

Ferreira, N.(1993) *Cidadania: uma questão para a educação.* Rio de Janeiro, Nova Fronteira.

Osler, A. and Starkey, H. (1996) *Teacher Education and Human Rights.* London: David Fulton.

Osler, A., and Starkey, H. (2003) Learning for cosmopolitan citizenship: theoretical debates and young people's experiences, *Educational Review,* 55(3): 243-254.

Parker, W.C.; Ninomiya, A. and Cogan, J. (1999). Educating world citizens: toward multinational curriculum development, *American Educational Research Journal,* 36 (2): 117-145.

Severino, A. (1994) *Filosofia da Educação: construindo a cidadania.* São Paulo: FTD.

Smith, A. Global challenges for citizenship education. Available at <http://www.global-citizenship.org/pdf/research/Alan%20Smith%20-%20Global%20Challen.pdf.(Accessed 5 March, 2004).

Starkey, H. (2002) *Democratic Citizenship, Languages, Diversity and Human Rights.* Strasbourg, Council of Europe.

UNESCO (1974) *Recommendation concerning Education for International Understanding.* Paris: UNESCO.

UNESCO (1995) *Declaration and Integrated Framework of Action on Education for Peace, Human Rights and Democracy.* Paris: UNESCO.

Contributors

Vanessa Andreotti is a Brazilian educator who works with citizenship and development education in the UK and is currently undertaking a PhD in the field of education and critical theory at Nottingham University.

Margot Brown is National Coordinator of the Centre for Global Education at York St John College.

Teresa Cañas Davis is Rector of IES Lenguas Vivas 'Juan R. Fernandez' and General Coordinator of the Multilingual Schools Programme, City of Buenos Aires, Argentina.

Kip Cates teaches in the Faculty of Regional Sciences of Tottori University, Japan and edits the Global Issues in Language Education Newsletter.

Dolores Corona Is Professor of English at the University of Havana and ELT advisor at the Ministry of Higher Education of the Republic of Cuba.

Telma Gimenez is Associate Professor, Department of Foreign Languages at Universidade Estadual de Londrina, Brazil.

Audrey Osler is Professor of Education and Director of the Centre for Citizenship and Human Rights Education at the University of Leeds.

Christopher Palmer is Deputy Director, British Council Seminars, Oxford.

Tuula Penttilä is Vice-principal and teacher of English and Swedish at Mankkaa School in Espoo, Finland.

Ruxandra Popovici is English Language Projects Manager at the British Council, Bucharest, Romania.

Robin Richardson is a director of the Insted Educational Consultancy, London.

Hugh Starkey is Senior Lecturer and course leader for the MA in Education (Citizenship/History) by distance learning at the University of London, Institute of Education.

Citation Index

Subject Index